GRANDMOTHERS WHO INSPIRED US ACROSS THE WORLD

A Collection of 31 Memoirs

Author, Collector and Editor
Merry Adler

Illustrator
Natasha de Francisco

Marble House Editions

Published by Marble House Editions

67-66 108th Street (Suite D-27)

Forest Hills, NY 11375

elizabeth.uhlig7@gmail.com

www.marble-house-editions.com

LCC Cataloguing-in-Publication Data

Adler, Merry

Grandmothers Who Inspired Us Across The World –

A Collection of 31 Memoirs/by Merry Adler

Summary: A compilation of reminiscences by grown grandchildren about their strong bond and positive influence of their grandmothers.

www.merryadlerbooks.com

ISBN 978-0-9966224-4-8

LCC Card Number 2018949370

Production Date: November 2018

Plant & Location   Printed by Everbest Printing Co. Ltd., Nansha, CHINA

Job & Batch #: 82143

DEDICATION

To Nana, my maternal grandmother, Rose Klein Friedenberg, who was my greatest inspiration. It was Nana, hands down, who had the most positive influence on my life.

To grandmothers across the world, your legacies of unwavering love and inspiration live on in the hearts and minds of your grandchildren.

To Carole Sue Smith, my dearest friend, wife, mother, grandmother and (sister), who died on November 10, 2015.

ACKNOWLEDGMENTS

To all my 30 contributors, I thank you for providing us with your warmest memories, respect and ongoing inspiration from your grandmothers. Without your recollections – both happy and sad, funny and serious, heart-warming and heart-wrenching, there would be no opportunity for our unique memoirs to be shared by many.

To Margaret Diehl, my editor, coach and teacher. I thank you for always being available to answer any and all questions and consistently guiding me throughout this remarkable journey.

To Natasha de Francisco, my uniquely talented, artistic illustrator who understood what I was looking for from our very first meeting.

PROLOGUE

In heartfelt reflection, my own maternal grandmother had the most powerful, positive influence on my life. No doubt, it was her consistent love, incredible inner strength and courage that propelled me to create this anthology. This book is a collection of 31 memoirs primarily from adult grandchildren who valued their grandmothers and who were inspired by them throughout their lives. Three grandchildren under the age of 10 and one teenager were proud to contribute as well. There are grandchildren who have written articles and descriptive, narrative essays about their grandmothers and there are a plethora of books proclaiming the joys of grandmotherhood. But I have not yet seen a collection such as this compendium that gathers a large number of heartfelt memoirs from the grandchild's voice to pen and paper.

To regress, over three decades ago, I visualized that I would write a memoir about my grandmother with her incredible backbone and spirit. Eventually, I could see that each chapter would belong to a grandmother which would provide a certain amount of demographic information for the reader. This collection started in 2014, and I made a calculated goal of how I would reach other dedicated grandchildren to speak about their grandmothers. I never wanted or needed to advertise for contributors as I thought these memoirs should be written with utmost honesty and pride. Further, I did not realize how many people I knew. Out of 31 contributors including myself, I knew 19 of them who were indeed qualified. The criteria was simple. I wanted to meet grandchildren who had loving, close relationships with their grandmothers. The remaining 12 were referrals from someone I knew or who were related to someone I knew. I also created a basic methodology for the contributors. Prior to meeting them, whether in person or on the phone, I discussesd the goals of this journey that I had also set for myself. A host of questions were sent to these contributors, in advance, after our first conversation, and my role as collector and editor of these memoirs moved along.

I have long believed and witnessed in my career that grandparents and elders, in general, are often undervalued in our society. These memoirs prove that a grandmother's love can have a strong and positive effect on her grandchild. A good, loving grandmother is no different whether she lives in Mississippi or Morocco. The languages of these grandmothers, their culture and religions may vary *but their love is the same.*

These skillfully detailed memoirs reveal some examples of children who were affected by war. In one instance, a British grandchild states that as World

War II approached, her sister was born. As German bombs started to fall on Liverpool – particularly on the docks of the huge shipping port, about two or three miles away, this grandchild was sent to live with her grandmother who lived about 20 miles north in a seaside town called Southport.

Generations affect people who are also influenced by their own experiences. Another grandmother was born in Georgia, part of the Soviet Union at that time, where *her* mother had to escape turbulent times of the new Post-Revolutionary Era. This grandmother lived through many hardships, deprivations, reforms, losses, deaths and wars. Her grandchild proudly writes that these things cemented her grandmother's character forever and made her tough and resistant. She wrote of her, "A tiny lady with a piercing look of her ice-blue eyes. The look that could reverse tides, open any doors and make mountains speak."

The youngest grandchild, age seven, expresses her love for her late grandmother, while a 90-year-old grandchild vividly recalls her loving grandmother with such tenderness as if she was that young grandchild today.

Each chapter is devoted to a grandmother and some were lucky enough to have loving memories with both of their grandmothers. Also included is her name, the nickname each grandchild called his or her grandmother, origin of birth, maternal or paternal, date of birth and/or death. All the grandchildren but one, offer the reader a photo or two of his or her grandmother and provide his or her name and location at the end of each chapter.

One third of these grandmothers were born in 10 countries outside the United States: China, Colombia (South America), France, Italy, Mexico, Russia, Sweden, Syria, the United Kingdom and Vietnam.

The common thread throughout this collection is the strong bond and enlightening relationship between grandmother and grandchild. While some stories reveal tragedies, triumph ultimately prevails as these grandmothers had incredible fortitude, spirit and wisdom. Such strong qualities are permanently left in the hearts and minds of their grandchildren.

Merry Adler

Our World of Grandmothers

United States of America

United Kingdom

Sweden

France

Italy

Russia

China

Vietnam

Syria

Colombia

Mexico

TABLE OF CONTENTS

CHAPTER I   Rose A. Klein Friedenberg 1

CHAPTER II   Victoria Long Cox 11

CHAPTER III Carolyn Driscoll Hoyt 15

CHAPTER IV Louise Johnson Wesley 21

           Rosa Victoria Jones Holloman 28

CHAPTER V Michelina Arcaro 33

CHAPTER VI Madeleine Perris, born Madeleine Gironce 39

           Jeanne Marsaud, born Jeanne Moreau 43

CHAPTER VII Carole Sue Smith 47

CHAPTER VIII Josephine (Jo) Guasto Belizzone 53

CHAPTER IX Minnie Annette Hill Wilkins 61

CHAPTER X Mary Caruso 67

CHAPTER XI Grace Francis Weaver 73

           Anita Valero 77

CHAPTER XII Rose A. Klein Friedenberg 81

CHAPTER XIII Margaret Lucille King Spillane 85

CHAPTER XIV Henrietta Wilhemina Christina Miller Schmidt .. 91

CHAPTER XV Kezia Mary (Payne) Guffey 97

CHAPTER XVI Jeannette Louise Koster Detweiler Latham 105

CHAPTER XVII Pearl Magda Hughey White 111

CHAPTER XVIII Molly Horowitz 117

     Mary Elisa Maruca 120

CHAPTER XIX Clara V. Chaudoin Porter 123

CHAPTER XX Marie Lavigne 129

CHAPTER XXI Ruby Camilla Tabor McCarty 133

CHAPTER XXII Florence Maud Goulden 139

CHAPTER XXIII Astrid Elena Guerrero Portillo 145

CHAPTER XXIV Mary Geha 149

CHAPTER XXV Elizabeth Mary Viscosi 153

CHAPTER XXVI Maria Kathryn Martin McCormick 159

CHAPTER XXVII Eliza Springer 165

CHAPTER XXVIII Pattama Phanphensophon 169

     Tsui Bik King 172

CHAPTER XXIX Edna Barth Barrows 173

CHAPTER XXX Maja Elisabet 179

CHAPTER XXXI Vera Bogomolova 187

CHAPTER I

Nana, my grandmother,
my inspiration

Merry and Nana

Rose A. Klein Friedenberg

Date of Birth: June 1, 1893 – Date of Death: February 6, 1976

Maternal Grandmother

Nana

No one had a grandmother like mine. Absolutely no one - with the exception of her other eight grandchildren. The nine of us called her 'Nana' and she was always there for all of us. My grandmother was pragmatic, unassuming, positive, and ever so courageous throughout her entire life. She was about five foot three with deep brown eyes, gray, curly, short hair and a prominent, narrow nose. My sister was the first grandchild; and I, the third. Her own four children loved her very much. I knew each of them and know this to be true. This says a lot about a mother's love, my grandmother's love.

Nana was also ageless, tolerant of all religions and races, and extremely modern for her time. She had a keen interest in learning all her life. At age 64, she took Spanish lessons because her bilingual daughter-in-law, a native Argentine, married Nana's only son. It was important for Nana that she was able to converse with her two bilingual grandchildren. I remember my grandmother's Spanish accent was unbearable, but not many grandparents have the courage to learn another language in their mid-sixties.

Nana was a first generation American. Both her mother and father were born in Hungary, during the Austrian-Hungarian Empire. They came to the United States to start a new life. Nana was the youngest of four children; the first was a son, and the following three were girls. She did not finish high school and had to work to make money because her father left her mother and the family. Nana grew up in Elizabeth, New Jersey, and married my grandfather, Samuel Friedenberg, when she was 21 years of age. Grandpa Sam came to this country with his mother who had lived on the edge of the Polish frontier with East Prussia. They joined his father in America, in 1893, when Sam was seven years of age.

After all these years, I can still hear Nana's voice with clarity. While she has been deceased for over 40 years, her spirit and enduring love remain with me. As a child, I remember when she and Grandpa visited my family in West Hartford, Connecticut. My father took home-made movies of all of us, in both black and white and color that spanned close to two decades. They have always captured my full attention. I love to see family footage of yesteryear and many happy times. We also had many Passovers with my grandparents in their Connecticut house and Thanksgivings with both sides of the family.

My grandparents lived in many homes in New York City and in 1946, Grandpa purchased a 12-acre estate in Greenwich, Connecticut when I was three years old. Nana, her children and their children, my sibling and cousins provided me the foundation of family and stability in my formative years, adolescence and beyond into the present day, long after her death. The Greenwich house was my grandparents' summer home, high on a hill, overlooking Long Island Sound. They had their own private beach and I can still smell and hear the tide.

Nana and I sat countless times on those distinctive sharp, gray, granite rocks that are native to that part of the state. We talked about everything on those rocks. The rocks were everywhere as if they were gatekeepers to Nana's home. They were lined up on both sides of her winding road, down by the beach, near the dock, near her gazebo that overlooked the sound and not far from her tall flag pole. When I didn't drive but occasionally flew to see her, I could easily identify her home because of that very tall, white pole. Those rocks always gave me a sense of calm, love, security, and reminded me of fun with Nana. When I was very young I was frightened by the horseshoe crabs that were left on the shore at low tide. I recall my uncle telling me that these crabs dated back nearly 450 million years – way before dinosaurs. I presume they are the original Greenwich residents and not leaving any time soon.

There was also a stately castle on the property, which was part of the estate. Nana and my uncle gave me the history of Whitney Castle. Mr. Whitney, a Broadway producer, bought the property in 1910. He modeled it after the Blarney Castle in Ireland but then fell on hard times and sold it to a buyer in 1922, after having never completed it. Nana said that the new owner had all of the stonework shipped from Scotland covering the entire exterior frame and that it was indeed completed before it was sold to my grandfather in 1946. I still have a photo of that castle taken of one of my very young cousins sitting near this gigantic, majestic fortress.

I vividly remember playing in one part of the castle, the music room, that was circular in shape, draped in ivy on its exterior, and inside, the walls had the most beautiful honey-colored wood paneling. Nana also told me time and time again that Grandpa wanted the family to live *in* the castle. But she said, "Sam, we are going to live *in* the Victorian house up on the hill." And so, they did.

I remember the huge, ancient beech tree that sat fairly near Nana's house and a bit farther from the beach itself. It resembled a weeping willow, and my sister, our cousins and I would play hide-and-seek inside that tree. Those thick, gnarly branches were fun to climb, and the leaves made me feel protected and hidden from the outside world. I have photos of my sister and me standing in front of that tree when I was about five years old. I also have photos of me standing in front of that same tree, some 52 years later, with my cousins and their children.

When I was young, Nana's three daughters and their children stayed with her during the summer months. I remember being in that house with my mother, sister and another cousin. It was a perfect arrangement for family to be together. For fun, my sister and I laid down, stretched out, and rolled ourselves down the long, grassy hill in front of Nana and Grandpa's house. Then we went back up and then back down a lot. This majestic piece of land ultimately led to the beach area. Its scenic views will forever remain in my memory. The estate also had a huge brown barn adjacent to a home, which was across the other side of the road. There were horses there at one point, but they were not there for long after Grandpa bought the estate. My mother's elder sister lived in the house for a short period.

To understand why my grandmother meant so much to me, you must know that her daughter, my mother, died at 49 years of age. Nana was 72 years of age at that time. I was 11 years old and my sister was 14 when our 38-year old mother was diagnosed with an insidious disease. I was 22 years old when she eventually closed her eyes for the last time. She was bedridden for over seven years, the last year in a nursing home, incapable of doing the most mundane things we do every day without thinking. Nana outlived two daughters, and ironically, both at the age of 49, two sons-in-law and a husband, my grandfather, by nearly 20 years.

Nana and Grandpa shared a life and lifestyle that was anything but ordinary. Both Nana and Grandpa traveled to Europe a few times as well as taking a trip to Havana, Cuba, in 1934 with two of their younger children. I thought all grandmothers lived like mine until I grew older, left home for college and realized how I was indeed very wrong. Grandpa Sam was the quintessential ambitious young man and without any formal education. Sadly, I remember very little about him but recall the day he died, when I was 13 years old. There are books written about my grandfather because he was not only extraordinarily successful, he was extremely philanthropic and his cultural interests and contributions were endless. Grandpa was both intellectual and a very successful businessman, which is a rare find in one person. Nana and my uncle said he was quiet, methodical and always made the right decisions.

Grandpa was born ambitious. At fourteen years of age, attending evening high school, he worked for his cousin who was a thread merchant. At 21 years of age, he entered business for himself in New York City, founding the Samuel Friedenberg Company, a thread manufacturing firm. While that business failed, he became the owner of the Freemont Thread Company, and served as its President. In addition, he founded the Arrow Yarn Dying Corporation, in New York City, which supplied dyes for the Freemont Thread Company. In 1919, at age 33, he sold both businesses, entered the real estate business and became president of the John Platt Realty Corporation.

Grandpa built, owned and sold commercial and residential real estate all over Manhattan. Many of the properties were located in the financial sector, near Wall Street. In 1930, he built a 30-story building and despite the Great Depression, it was profitable. In 1952, he built a 25-story building, and it was also a success. My grandparents were Republican and Jewish, which in some ways could be called an oxymoron, especially in that era. Grandpa had a variety of interests and acquisitions, including a collection of 100 fine paintings. He was a benefactor of The New York Botanical Garden.

Another interest was revealed by the acquisition of reputedly the largest collection of Jewish medallions and plaques in the world. In 1948, he presented more than 1500 pieces of this collection to The Jewish Museum in New York City, of which he was a trustee. The accolades and contributions are way too numerous to mention, but I will always feel proud.

I remember that whether in Connecticut or New York City, Nana, her children and their children, at every meal, engaged in discussions about art, theater, politics, books, music, film, what exhibit was being shown and where, etc. Everyone jumped in with their opinions, some more passionate than others. My uncle loved to debate and always challenged us, regardless of which side we were defending. I loved the energy from Nana and my mother's family; I never had anything like that in my own home growing up. These conversations continued well after Nana passed away and trickled down from my aunt and uncle to their children and my cousins. In a way, I still feel Nana's presence and love when I am with my mother's family.

Wherever Nana lived, her homes always had beautiful paintings, Persian rugs, antiques everywhere, large Jade Bonsai plants, her pianos, books and comfortable furniture. I can still hear Nana saying, "Things can always be replaced but not people." Her hallways were always adorned with many family photos wherever she lived, and I've copied her ever since I started living on my own.

I never felt that Nana was my mother. I am told their personalities were entirely different. Nana was on the short side and always said she thought grandmothers should be a little plump. Nana moved quickly while my mother was fairly tall, calm, quieter and perhaps a little more intellectual. She was often mistaken for the British actress, Greer Garson. Another one of Nana's favorite adages was, "You can have many fathers but only one mother." She and I talked about my mother a lot. What better person to ask? I always had many questions and she answered them all. She also saved the letters my mother wrote her when she was in college and when married. To this day, I love reading them; the joy in reading my mother's words makes me feel as if I am getting to know her for the first time. Nana saved many mementos that each of her four children made for her so that her grandchildren could pass them on to their children. Nana and I wrote to each other for years and I have saved each and every letter.

As my mother's illness progressed and as she could not speak, walk or eat without assistance, Nana visited my mother more than anyone else in the family, on either side of the family or any of my mother's friends. She drove from Greenwich or New York City, alone which was at least a four-hour drive. The last year of my mother's life was spent in a nursing home in rural Connecticut and Nana made those regular trips as well. I remember asking her if she ever cried as I never saw her shed a tear. Her answer was always the same, "Only when I am alone." She truly believed in living life "in the present" and my greatest present was Nana. I feel very lucky that my relationship with her truly developed when I was a young adult, so I remember her clearly. However, I am also grateful that I had my own beautiful, healthy mother in those formative years when I may have needed her the most.

I really don't know if Nana was a good or great cook. Our conversations always overshadowed her culinary talents. She was a great hostess and

I recall many beautiful meals that Nana provided for friends and family – especially in Greenwich. She always had help, but she did make the best barley soup and everything else when I saw her in New York City. I do remember she made a great coffee cake in Connecticut that all of us loved. Mildred was the name of one of her cooks and when I was young, I saw her in Greenwich. She was from Scotland and made the best Scotch shortbread ever! I also remember the way Nana made a salad by only cutting very large chunks of lettuce, tomatoes and white radishes from her garden and beautifully arranging them on one of her platters. Her favorite color was green; maybe that was why she loved green, sour plums. So did I. Nana always played Beethoven's "Moonlight Sonata" for me, whether in Connecticut or in her apartment, in the city. I will always think of her when I hear that beautiful piece.

Nana was also my mentor. She believed in self-respect first and would tell me, "There is a healthy, selfish love and that should be yourself, first." We talked a lot about that subject; I can't remember not knowing what she meant. She used to say if we don't love ourselves, we cannot love another person. Of course she was right. She loved and respected herself, and you could feel it when you met her for the first time or whenever you interacted with her. She had a very strong, pragmatic personality yet was upbeat and loving at the same time. She always had her arms held wide and a hug waiting for me in Connecticut, as I drove up her long driveway or in New York City, standing by her open door as I left the elevator on her floor.

Like all wonderful grandmothers, Nana's family was her life. When I asked her about her children, what they were like when young, she would always say that you never know what personality your child will have and in many ways, "It's all in the stars." She remarked that each child of hers was entirely different. I remember conversations in her apartment when she would ask me about my life, what I was doing, was I reading Shakespeare, was I staying trim, eating right, was I meeting a nice man, etc. Nana was ageless and my friend as well as my grandmother. In my late twenties, I recall her leaving the keys to her Park Avenue apartment as I told her a friend of mine and I wanted to come into the city. She remained in Greenwich and trusted me entirely.

She believed in a strong work ethic and the value and personal reward of "giving back." When Grandpa Sam was alive, she would go downtown to the Financial District once a week and sit with the telephone operators in one of Grandpa's buildings. She always respected people who worked hard and I have followed that same belief throughout my career. I have some of her traits today and while I do not look like any of my mother's family, I am fairly short as she was the only short person on both sides of my family. I too move quickly, am full of energy, gregarious and always optimistic.

Time and time again, Nana wanted me to know the difference between giving a gift and a loan. She emphasized if it was a loan, no matter how small, I would have to pay her back. She was so generous with every one of her nine grandchildren. To this day, all of us have many things that were hers and my grandfather's such as antiques, china, silver, crystal, jewelry, art, rugs and beautiful sconces, which came from the castle. She is everywhere in my home and always in my heart.

Nana was curious about the world and pursued whatever it was she wanted to learn. She attended lectures at The New School for Social Research when she was in her her seventies. She read a lot and adored New York City, the noise and the life in a city that never sleeps. After a few days in Greenwich, when all the grandchildren went home, she would say, "The house is too quiet, too neat, and too empty." She then left for the city, to her other home, which in some ways was very much like her-- full of life, a stimulating pulse and offered many venues to explore one's intellectual appetite. I can relate, as I too prefer living in the city than in the suburbs where I was raised as a child. It was never an imposition if I had an extra friend coming for lunch to either of Nana's homes. With effortless ease, she would put another placemat on the dining room table. It was always a non-issue.

When I visited Nana in the city, we went to the movies, went to see a play, had ice cream sundaes at Schraffts, or walked and looked at the storefronts. She adored Fifth Avenue, and always said how everyone should be in New York City at Christmas time. Once we walked out of a movie and laughed so hard thinking each wanted to stay when the opposite was true.

On one of my visits to Greenwich, Nana wanted me to drive her to the family cemetery in Westchester County. She wanted to put flowers on the tombstones of both my grandfather and my mother. I remember how hard this was for me as it must have been for my grandmother. I actually asked her to give me a few minutes alone by my mother's grave. She understood and obliged but when she returned, I remember her saying, with her throat cracking a little, "Don't cry for me when I am gone, Merry...I have had a very good, full life, and I know you will be all right." The strange part about this is that whenever I think of Nana, I never cry. I do still cry for my mother.

As everyone has a last day on earth, it happened for Nana at 82 years of age. Nana had renal failure and was admitted to a hospital in Manhattan, in the Intensive Care Unit (ICU). Nana gave me many gifts and one of them was a gold leaf pin with a stem made of diamonds. Her first child, my mother's older sister, also lived in Manhattan and she called me to let me know that Nana was in and out of consciousness. But Nana was upset about something and finally, my aunt understood what Nana was saying. She thought I sold the pin she gave me a long time ago! Of course, I have the pin to this day.

I was living in Boston at that time and I immediately flew to New York City and spent the day in the ICU sitting next to Nana. I remember sitting on her bed, on her right side, and she was moving and speaking somewhat coherently. Her eyes were shut, but I took her hand and put it on my pin and told her, "Nana, it is Merry. I am here. I have your hand touching that beautiful pin you gave me. I *never* sold it." I told her I loved her and that I was so lucky to have her in my life. I know she knew it was me, and she knew I did not sell her beautiful pin. Nana passed away the very next day.

I always wanted to be a mother and to pass down to my grandchildren what my maternal grandmother did for me. But it was not my destiny. I look back and know how lucky I was to have had my grandmother, Nana, for 32 years of my life. Her positivity and strength will remain with me for the rest of my days. Nana was right once again when she said, "You can always replace a thing but you can never replace a person." My mother's greatest gift to me was her mother - her mother's greatest gift to me was my mother.

Merry Adler
Washington, DC

CHAPTER II

Grandmama

Victoria Long Cox

Date of Birth: January 16, 1895 – Date of Death: August 7, 1986

Paternal Grandmother

Grandmama

My grandmother was born in Horry County, South Carolina, just 30 years after the end of the Civil War. Her ancestors had been plantation owners, and many of her relatives' lives were lost in battle.

Among her ancestors were two signers of the U.S. Constitution, yet she seemed to have no knowledge of this. I only discovered it while doing a genealogical search about one year ago.

She was known in the community as a saint and a poet. She was a pillar of the Baptist Church, and the faded pages of poetry within the vast family bible gave clues of a life beyond the Depression-era farm life of grinding poverty she endured.

The dexterity of her fingers in crocheting thousands of miles of intricate needlework betrayed a lost identity. An identity that a worshipful granddaughter would one day uncover: that of a Southern aristocrat.

Her garden full of flowers, the insistence of pressing on every visitor a lovely bouquet to take home with them; the generosity of spirit that all of this revealed was the legacy she left me.

She held me lovingly in her lap during the late 1950's reading the 23rd Psalm to me. And that Psalm remains intertwined in my life today despite the passage of over 50 years.

When she died in August, 1986, I had been married only three months to a man who was a prince in every respect. This pleased her immensely. She felt she could watch my life unfold from her heavenly opera box. When the news of her death reached me, I felt as though half the sun's wattage had been taken forever after.

The first time I saw her favorite flower – a blue hydrangea – after her death, I felt she was trying to communicate with me. It kept happening. Grandmama's messages. "I love you. Don't despair, use your life as I did: to love, serve, and leave beauty in your wake."

Victoria Buresch
Washington, DC

CHAPTER III

Mai and Charlotte

Carolyn Driscoll Hoyt

Date of Birth: September 20, 1927 – Date of Death: December 6, 2015

Maternal Grandmother

Mai

My name is Charlotte Bradstreet Key, and many people call me 'Charlie.' I am 14 years old, and I was born in Bangkok, Thailand. I often used to go to the U.S. in the summer to visit my grandmother and aunts. I live in the beautiful city of Harrogate, which is located in North Yorkshire, England, which is a four-hour drive from London or close to two hours by train.

Mai was young and 'hip' and did not want to be called 'grandma' or anything like that, so she chose the name Mai, which is the Portuguese word for 'mother' and is pronounced 'my.'

I have two brothers, William and Henry, and a sister, Caroline, so there are four of us in total. When Mai was young, her mother died of cancer when she was 14 and a freshman in high school. When she was 17 and a senior in high school, Mai's father died of cancer. Her aunt, 'Big C,' and older sister Barbara, who was 19 at the time, took care of Mai and her younger sister, Sally.

My mother, who I call 'Mama' and my dad helped me with the information about Mai when she was younger and way before I was born. Mai was born in Omaha, Nebraska, but left after graduating from high school. During her life, Mai lived in many places all over the world. Mai went to Bradford College in Massachusetts for two years. She then transferred to Cal, University of California at Berkeley, as it was known then. Mai then went to Tobe-Coburn in New York City to study advertising; she then moved to San Francisco and worked as the Director of Advertising at Joseph Magnin, a high-end department store. Mai was well known in San Francisco, and that was where she met her husband, Howard Henry Hoyt III. The two then moved to Panama where Mai gave birth to her first daughter, Carolina. Then they moved to Puerto Rico where she gave birth to twins, Louisa, who is my mom, and Sarah. The family then moved to Bethesda, Maryland; Miami, Florida; Madrid, Spain; Lisbon, Portugal and finally Frederick, Maryland, where Mai lived for 35 years and loved it! Mai decided to downsize and be closer to my aunts, so she moved to a beautiful apartment in Washington, DC.

'The South of France' was what Mai called her basement; the walls were covered with murals that were copies of the work of the famous painter Cezanne and decorated in a manner that made it look as if you were actually in Provence, the South of France. The murals were painted by an up-and-coming art student at Hood College in Frederick, Maryland, where Mai worked 30+ years. Mai loved the South of France and traveled there many times.

My earliest memories of Mai are through the photos that were taken on my first birthday. My actual first memory of Mai was at her house when I was two years old, chasing fireflies with Mai, my brothers and sister; I had never seen fireflies before.

Mai was 5'10" and always slim. As she got older, she started to 'shrink,' and her back was a little bent but not too much. Mai's reddish-brown hair was always perfect; she went to the beauty salon every week. Our family moved around a lot for my dad's work, and we always moved as a family. We spent a lot of time with Mai, and she would give us hugs and kisses any time she saw us. When we would wake up we always got lots of hugs and kisses; when we went to sleep, we would get hugs and kisses. Mai loved listening to people and loved to speak about experiences she'd had and finding out how everyone was doing.

Sometimes Mai would bake things with us, but she really preferred throwing parties and making a lot of big meals such as Thanksgiving Dinner, 4th of July picnics and birthdays. Any occasion was worth a party. My mother now has Mai's recipes, and she will pass them on to my sister, brothers and me.

The dollhouse I have now is a replica of the family home that Mai's father built in Omaha, Nebraska, and which Mai lived in until she graduated from high school. Mai's father had the dollhouse made for his three daughters; Mai, her older sister, Barbara, and younger sister, Sally, spent many hours playing with the dollhouse in their playroom.

When Mai took us to summer day camps we were living in Saigon, Vietnam; Ghana, and the UK. Since we lived abroad, we tended to switch summer visits between Mai in the United States and Grandad, my paternal grandfather, in the UK.

When in the United States, Mama, my brothers, sister and I all played together and were happy in the South of France (Mai's basement). When

I was around Mai, I felt nothing could go wrong; I felt happier every time I saw Mai. She would always take us to the Frederick Community College (FCC) for summer day camps, and we would see her big smile at the end of each day. When we all stood outside on the 4th of July, watching the fireworks on her rooftop terrace, that has to be my best memory with Mai. The fireworks were beautiful, and we all had face paint on – it was just amazing!

Mai also taught us to ride a bike – holding on to the bike with Mai running behind. She took us for swimming lessons, went for walks and taught us how to organize a successful lemonade stand which we had never done before. Sometimes we used to read and do homework in Mai's glassed-in sunroom, which was filled with sofas and comfy chairs and where we would sometimes have meals. All of this looked out onto her beautiful garden, which had a brick terrace and a big wrought-iron table and many chairs where we would eat corn on the cob; it reminded Mai a lot of when she a little girl in Omaha.

Mai loved to travel, and she went to so many places and had so much fun doing things like dog sledding in Alaska; hot air ballooning in Burma; clambering the ruins of Angkor Wat in Cambodia; entering the Cu Chi tunnels in Vietnam, jet skiing in Koh Chang, Thailand; exploring Hong Kong; discovering penguins and icebergs in Antarctica; fighting windmills in Spain; wandering, amazed, through the ruins in Mexico; having picnics every weekend in Portugal; discovering Central and South America. There was nowhere Mai would not go…

Mai's house always smelled so nice and had a homey smell too. We all really miss Mai so very much, and I wish that she could have stayed on earth with my entire family.

Mai died at the age of 88 in Washington, D.C. She lived, she loved, she was loved, and she had children and grandchildren. She had a long, eventful, wonderful life. I wrote a poem that was read at Mai's memorial service in December 2015. In the poem, the fireflies represented when we all went out at night to catch fireflies, and it is also talking about Mai. It has two meanings so in the end, when it says now we finally say goodbye to these beautiful fireflies, it is talking about Mai leaving us, but she is still in our family's hearts forever.

Light
Late at night
When there's no light,
The fireflies come out to play
For it is no longer the day,
They dance and flicker across the bright moon
While the crickets play their sweet, sweet tune,
They shimmer and glitter in the trees
And in the flowers because there aren't bees.
Now we finally say goodbye
To these beautiful fireflies,
Late at night
When there's no light,
The fireflies come out to play
For it is no longer the day.

If I could sum up Mai, it would be 'amazing,' and she had a 'giant heart.' I asked my mother, and she said Mai was "smart, kind, humble, had much humility and was very courageous."

If I could say anything to Mai, now, I would say, "I love you and miss you and hope you are happy and having fun with your family and friends in heaven."

Charlotte Bradstreet Key
United Kingdom

CHAPTER IV

Granna

Mama

Photo below:

Mama and her husband,

Rev, John Holloman

Louise Johnson Wesley

Date of Birth: December 27, 1895 – Date of Death: March 15, 1973

Maternal Grandmother

Granna

There was nothing stereotypical about my African American grandparents. I knew all four of them very well. They helped to raise me. They were kind and gentle people, honest, hardworking, and solidly middle class. They taught me humility and responsibility among whatever better personal qualities I may have. In the context of their time and place, I'm proud and grateful to have had them as family and as role models.

My maternal grandmother's name was Louise Johnson Wesley. I called her "Granna". She was the second to the eldest of the six daughters of Charles Snowden Johnson, the first African American podiatrist in Baltimore, Maryland. My grandmother's census classification was "Mulatto". She was a young socialite and school teacher when she married my grandfather, Charles Harris Wesley, in 1913. He had just received a Master's degree from Yale University, uncommon for an African American man at that time. They made their home in Washington, DC where they had two daughters. The eldest by seven years, Louise, was sickly from a young age and died in 1950 at 35. The other, Charlotte, my mother, passed away in 2015 at 93.

My grandfather, "Granddaddy", taught Economics and History at Howard University in Washington, DC, and became dean of the graduate school there. He bought a house near the university where my mother grew up. She lived with her parents until she finished college at Howard and moved to New York to attend graduate school at Columbia University. In 1930, Granddaddy received a Guggenheim Fellowship for study abroad and the family lived in London for a year.

Granna could play the piano, and Granddaddy could sing. In college, he had been a member of the Fisk Jubilee Singers, the famed men's choral group which still exists today. Consequently, both of their daughters were born musically gifted, and became accomplished pianists. Granna made sure they got the necessary training and exposure, with regular music lessons, concerts and recitals. In college, my mother, Charlotte, switched her major from piano to voice and became a renowned opera singer and later a classical music and vocal arts educator, and a private vocal coach. Granna excelled at being a stage mother. She loved the role and was so proud of her girls.

I knew my grandmother the longest and the best when she was living in Wilberforce, Ohio where my grandfather, who had also earned a PhD from Harvard University in 1925, was an author of African American history books and monographs, and a college president. He was the president of Wilberforce University in the early 1940's, and then was the moving force and founding president of Central State College, now Central State University, built on land adjacent to Wilberforce. Both schools catered primarily to the higher education needs of African Americans, in those days called Negroes or Coloreds. Granna and Grandddaddy lived in the president's house, a seven-bedroom mansion on the school's large and beautiful campus. Granna was the first lady of the college.

They lived in Ohio from before I was born until my grandfather retired back to DC in 1965 when I was 19 years old. Granna passed away in DC eight years later. I lived with my parents in New York City, was an only child, and the only Wesley grandchild. I understood that I was privileged and spoiled in the best ways of ways. Every year until I was nine, my parents would drive me to spend summers with my Granna in Wilberforce, which was located three miles from Xenia, 15 miles from Antioch College in Yellow Springs, and 18 miles from Dayton.

My grandparents were raising one of her sister's granddaughters, my cousin Olga Ellis, who was my age. I loved to go Ohio to visit because it was a lush, traffic-free environment, and because there was always someone there for me to play with. They had a dog, a chow mix named Fluffy. There was a swing set on the grounds of the house, a large vegetable garden, and a gardener with a golf cart. He planted flowers and landscaped the property around the house and the grounds of the surrounding campus. Granna let me walk all around the campus by myself, ride on the golf cart, and work in the garden with my grandfather.

They grew several kinds of greens, berries, tomatoes, squash and corn in their garden. Granna fixed salads for lunch every day, and my grandfather would walk home from his office on campus to eat with us. Both were very health conscious, took several different vitamins, ate and drank lots of fruit and juices, and didn't vary much from their diets. We ate vegetables and broiled T-bone steak for dinner most evenings, with fresh chopped garlic on top, and sometimes chicken. They drank very little alcohol and didn't smoke cigarettes.

There were always one or two college students working in and around the house helping my grandmother with the household engineering. They were paid and received college credit. Some were from very poor families in rural southern communities, and one or two came from Africa. If they needed winter clothing, she sometimes gave away Granddaddy's. She also gave them extra money and guidance. Granna treated her students like they were her family, stayed in touch and was generous_ with them even after they graduated. I learned generosity, and what it means to be charitable, from watching my Granna.

During her entire marriage, my grandmother's mother-in-law, Matilda, also lived in the house with them, until her passing in 1962. They appeared to get along and stayed out of one another's way. Grandma Wesley was a seamstress who spent most of her time in her room on her sewing machine, and made all of her own clothes. Granna also loved to sew, and often made clothes for herself, and dressy clothes for her daughters, and for my cousin and me. She was a stylish woman who would make her own suits, and pillbox hats that sat in the middle of the top of her head before Jackie Kennedy made them famous. I remember a black velvet opera coat with rhinestone buttons that she made and then gave to my mother. She taught me how to sew, but I had no talent.

Granna had long, straight auburn hair which she fixed on top of her head and behind. I would watch her sit at her vanity table every morning and apply hairpins, rats, and chignons to create an elaborate and becoming hairstyle. She had patience and cared about her appearance.

My grandparents were interested in art, music, and literature. Granna would often give me books as gifts. The last book she gave me before she passed was the classic, "Things Fall Apart" by Chinua Achebe. There was a piano in the house, of course, and there was a room called the library with a large desk and chairs, and floor to ceiling barristers' bookcases. It served as Granddaddy's study, his man-cave. He spent most of his home time there and it was where other male visitors and "thinkers" from all over gathered to talk, smoke cigars and discuss timely social, political and religious matters.

Granna entertained a lot as well. There were regular visits and sleepovers from out of town family members, and she hosted dinners and receptions at her home for faculty, administrators, college trustees, Ohio state government officials, and assorted dignitaries from all over. Granddaddy, a bookworm and a writer, was socially inept. He loved sports, so the college had basketball, football and tennis teams. He would take me to their games. Granna had the interpersonal skills he lacked and she always protected him, made him look good and be more accessible.

She taught me how to be gracious, even to people I didn't like, and she taught me table etiquette and how to act in social settings. She was always very patient and loving and affectionate with me, and some of the warmer aspects of my own rather aloof personality came from her. She nursed me when I was sick or injured or in pain.

She could cook, too. She would bake the best rolls, and spoon bread, and lemon meringue pies made out of fresh lemons, lemon zest and condensed milk. Both she and my great-grandmother could cook. Unless one or the other of them decided to make something sweet, we didn't eat dessert. I learned how to cook from watching Granna, but I still don't enjoy baking.

Granna was also a collector. She collected fine costume jewelry, some of it in colorful rhinestone settings, and gave it to her daughters to wear with their gowns when they were performing. She was able to appreciate it from the audience. And, she collected other things, crystal, china, stemware, silverware, tea sets and table linens. She and my great-grandmother sometimes worked together, sewing, knitting and crocheting table lines and bedcovers. Granna would take me shopping with her to the nearest department store which was in Dayton, Ohio, and to have a sandwich in the restaurant. On the drive over and back, she would share her wisdom.

There were tragedies and sad moments in Granna's life. The disappearance from the family of her youngest sister whom she had helped to raise. The sister, Elizabeth, who was blond and very fair skinned, decided to separate from her family when she was a teenager to live as a white person. Granna would never talk to us about her even though Olga and I were very curious about the circumstances and why Elizabeth would want to do that. Others in our family were light-skinned and they didn't choose "pass" and "crossover". Olga and I have come to realize in recent years that not talking about Elizabeth and denying knowledge of her whereabouts was Granna's way of protecting her from being otherwise identified.

There was the death of her daughter from a debilitating disease. Medical science wasn't then what it is now, and the best care wasn't always available to Negroes. Aunt Louise suffered for a long time, was bedridden and died from the complications of something. Whatever, it wasn't successfully treated or cured. I was too young to measure Granna's grief.

Then in 1953, while driving back from Columbus, Granna and Granddaddy were in a very bad automobile accident and my Granna's ankle bone was broken in half. A truck driver had forced them off the road and over the side of a bridge. We never learned why, but we had our suspicions. The ankle never healed properly and the wound was always ugly and raw looking. At first, she walked with metal crutches with metal vice like arm grips and then with a cane, but she was maimed_for the rest of her life. I believe that injury and the ankle's failure to heal brought on the multiple myeloma cancer which she lived with silently for years, and which eventually killed her. She also suffered from osteoarthritis. Even though she regularly went to doctors, she went alone, and never let on to anyone how sick she was or the extent of her pain.

Granna taught me stoicism. She taught me how to bite the bullet and suffer in silence through all types of physical, emotional and psychological pain, and to do it with dignity. I count my blessings every single day that I had her in my life for as long as I did. She was a rock.

Rosa Victoria Jones Holloman

Date of Birth: November 7, 1888 – Date of Death: March 15, 1975

Paternal Grandmother

Mama

The things that seemed to mean the most to my grandmother Holloman were her husband, her family, her church and her associations. She was one of five surviving daughters born to Robert Shelton Jones who had been enslaved. Through his labors, and against great odds, he became a landowner on Union Ridge in Charlottesville, in Albemarle County, Virginia. Her mother died giving birth to a younger sibling and her father's sister helped him to raise his girls. He insisted that they be educated and so they attended a school that had been built for Negroes after slaves were freed. Because Mama was a diligent student, her father encouraged her to enroll in college at Hampton Institute. It took her five years to get a degree because she worked in the school laundry to pay her tuition.

Rosa Victoria Jones Holloman was a person of tremendous faith. She had an aura of spirituality and contentment about her, and I was always comfortable in her presence. She could often be heard humming quietly to herself and was calm and even tempered, never yelling or screaming or given to any outward bursts of joy, anger or discomfort. She was completely unspoiled and genuine, humble and kind, and not in any way judgmental. Everyone liked her.

Mama first met Papa, my grandfather, her one true love and devoted life partner, at her job as a teacher at the Waters Normal Training Institute in Winton, NC. The Rev. John L. S. Holloman had graduated from Virginia Union University near Richmond, where he would later become the chair of the school's trustee board. Papa became a Baptist minister, and also taught math and Latin at Waters. They married in 1912.

In 1917, Papa was offered a position as Pastor of the Second Baptist Church in Washington, DC, and the family moved north. Papa served as pastor of this church for 53 years until his passing in 1970. He was the family's breadwinner. Mama was the homemaker and head of the household. They raised five children in a three-story townhouse they owned in the Shaw neighborhood of northwest DC not far from the church. Each of their offspring graduated from college and became accomplished, well-traveled, civic-minded individuals. Mama likewise helped to raise their children while her own were busy with their schooling and careers. All four daughters became professional educators among other endeavors.

Her only son, my father, became a physician and moved to Harlem in New York City where I was born. My parents, as well as his sisters, attended the same high school, the famed Paul Lawrence Dunbar HS in Washington, DC. For graduate studies my mother and father migrated to NYC where they later married. They would regularly drive down with me to DC to visit and sleepover at Mama and Papa's house. They sometimes left me with Mama when they were traveling on their own. Mama's home was the center of family activity, and aunts, and uncles, and cousins and visitors were always coming and going.

Mama did nearly all of the cooking for her family. She spent much of her time in the kitchen on the ground floor of the house in a chair at the sink by the window. Family came to the house to eat. Each year she hosted Thanksgiving dinner, and in late summer, Papa's Holloman Family reunions. Her daughters were her assistants. By watching and helping Mama, I learned how to cook and prepare meals. She made feeding large numbers of people look easy.

Mama and Papa always ate breakfast together before he left for the day. Very few words were spoken between them during this time. She seemed to naturally know what he wanted and needed. They were literally teetotalers, hot tea in the AM and iced tea with dinner in the PM. I can't recall ever seeing either of them drink any hard liquor or alcohol. Grape juice was served in church in place of wine on communion Sundays.

Mama could make the best chicken salad. She would boil the whole plucked chicken minus the head and feet, and then cut up everything but the bones and the cartilage. It was a rich and flavorful mixture even before she added anything else. She would cook baked goods, cookies and cupcakes for the church and for the various groups to which she belonged, and in which she held leadership positions.

Mama was active in many organizations including the Baptists Ministers' Wives, the Nurses' Aide Society, the Lott Carey Baptist Mission, and Datcher Chapter of the International Order of the Eastern Star.

At night when Papa returned home, however late it might be, he would sit by her bed and they would talk over all of the events of the day, and then say their prayers together on their knees. In her middle years, Mama developed severe rheumatoid arthritis in her legs. It was crippling and painful, but I never heard her complain. Over the years her legs became extremely bowed which made walking difficult. Every morning when she came down from the third floor to fix Papa's breakfast and begin her day, she didn't go back up those two flights of stairs until it was time to go to bed.

From Mama, I learned personal discipline by watching her regularly perform ordinary routine daily activities meant to serve and better the lives of her family and others. She and Papa travelled often to conventions and other gatherings intended for enrichment. They were once photographed on camels in front of the Great Pyramids of Giza as a part of their tour of the "Holy Land".

My parents didn't attend church regularly in New York City because they were so busy. But we always attended when we were in DC. I was a skeptic about God and religion. It was hard for me to understand the Bible, not just the language and phrasing. I was confused about who exactly had written and compiled all of the stories, and how it was done. Mama told me that the exact origin of the Bible wasn't as important as the stories it contained. They were history, she said, and they contained God's many lessons, and I should be looking to identify those lessons and to learn from them. She said she believed what was written, and that Papa was there to help me to better understand. Maybe I was six or seven years old.

In 1971, a year after Papa died, I moved to DC to finish college and attend graduate school. I visited Mama nearly every day to eat a meal with her and tell her of my activities. Mama was very lonely without Papa. She was sad all the time and the light had gone from her eyes. There was nothing I could do or say to cheer her up. Above all else, she had been Papa's partner and she was not the same without him. She became despondent a year later when her next best friend, her younger sister Nellie, died. Even though Mama had a large and attentive family, she said to me then that she was all alone. She meant that all of the loved ones of her generation had passed on.

Not long after that, she suffered a paralyzing stroke and had to move from her home to live with one of her daughters on the other side of the city, west of Rock Creek Park. She needed professional caregivers at that point. Her life as she had known it was effectively over. I was 28 years old when Mama passed.

Both of my grandmothers, Granna and Mama, died two years to the day from one another, on the Ides of March. Both are buried next to their husbands, not far from one another, in the same cemetery just outside of Washington, DC.

Charlotte Holloman

Charlotte is a retired educator, lawyer-lobbyist and public affairs consultant. In recent years, before their passing, she was caregiver for a close friend, two of her elderly Holloman aunts, and for her mother. She currently resides in Washington, DC.

CHAPTER V

Nonna

Michelina Arcaro

Date of Birth: September 3, 1895 – Date of Death: September 23, 1970

Maternal Grandmother

Nonna

My family is Italian on both sides. Each of my parents came from families of 10 children. Both families settled in Washington, DC, after arriving from Italy. During the 1950s, a lot of the children of immigrants tried to distance themselves from their ethnicity. My parents spoke Italian only when they didn't want me to understand what they were saying… never in public. This was a big part of the assimilation process, but they also needed to avoid discrimination. My dad would drop the "i" when speaking our last name, as a small example of this.

So against that backdrop, I would have the occasion, as each of my cousins did, to spend a few days at a time with Michelina Arcaro, "Nonna," my maternal grandmother. Born and raised in Viggiano, Italy, her world was still very Italian. Language, food, dress…I got immersed in an experience that felt both mysterious and comforting at the same time. Nonna was gentle and tough, unconditionally loving and the safest harbor ever for a little kid. She had 10 children (my mom, aunts and uncles), lost a son (Tony) in World War II, and her husband (Ralph) shortly after that.

Most of my communication with her was intuitive. She spoke only a little English, but I understood anything and everything she intended to communicate. Was my relationship with her special? It sure felt that way to me, but I'm also sure each of my cousins would share a similar recollection.

First and foremost, Nonna was PRESENT. She always showed up when it mattered. Births, deaths, people needing a meal or place to stay, she would show up, with whatever someone needed. No one was ever turned away from her home. To be that attentive and responsive, without having the ability to clearly communicate in English, was something I always found astounding. She raised 10 kids in a small DC row house and temporarily took in countless other kids in the neighborhood. Some of them are still alive and still expressing their gratitude. She was an artist when it came to crocheting. Afghans, beautifully intricate, lacy tablecloths and sweaters – she could spend hours doing this. Further, she taught my mom this same skill. Her cooking was simple, rustic and the best!   She could spend hours rolling out pasta dough for the best ravioli EVER! I have heard that in Italy, she also spent some time as a midwife.

Physically, I would describe her as stocky. She always wore a dress. To me, her face never changed or aged. If you ever saw a picture of an Italian grandmother on a box of pasta, it looked like my Nonna. She had a mole on her chin and massive arms that came from hours spent rolling pasta dough and pastries, doing house and yard work. There was a lucky squirrel that would scrape against the back screen door of her house. Nonna would feed that little guy by hand, and he came back every day for his treat. I can't remember exactly what she gave him to eat, but I'm guessing it was leftover Italian bread. I remember a time when she was visiting us, and my mom found a snake in the laundry room. Everyone ran but Nonna, who picked up a two-by-four and beat the snake until it died. All in a day's work!

Was she funny? Rarely intentionally. She was quiet and reserved, but when she would get upset, she could unleash a melodic stream of Italian curse words. When I was a little kid and would stay with her for a few days, I still had three bachelor uncles who lived with her. They were typical young men who would stay out late and then come home – sometimes inebriated. I remember being asleep and waking up to the sound of her yelling at them for being late. She'd call them "strunz" and some other names I can't spell. My uncles would later tell me the meaning of these words, and I felt like I had access to a secret code. Of course, they laughed at her yelling, and their laughter eventually caused her to laugh. She was loved by anyone who knew her.

Nonna died when I was 16, so my memories are largely impressionistic. Etched forever, though, are the smells that came from her kitchen. Garlic, onions, peppers, olive oil – those smells were always there, and to this day, when I walk into an Italian restaurant and that combination of smells is there, I immediately picture and recall Nonna. She would serve me food and then stand behind me while I ate. When the plate was empty, she'd add more food. If I slowed down or couldn't finish, I felt an affectionate tap on the side of my face, encouraging me to eat more. "Mangia, mangia," she would keep repeating. She could speak very little English, but she communicated her complete, unconditional love through food, hugs and cheek pinching.

A more surreal experience had to do with this language gap we had. I grew up hearing a lot of Italian from her but understanding and speaking next to none. I would always smile and nod my head when Nonna went on in Italian. When I was in my early 40s, my wife and I took a trip to Florence. My grandmother had been dead at least 25 years. We walked into a clothing store on the Ponte Vecchio, and there was an old woman working. It flashed on me that she resembled my grandmother. While I was shopping, another old woman walked in the store, but I never saw her. The shopkeeper asked a question in Italian to the woman who had just entered. I thought the question was directed to me, so I answered in Italian, which I cannot speak! I have no idea what the question was, but I am convinced that I must have heard the same question from my grandmother years earlier and somehow had logged the answer that must have come from someone else. Spooky.

Finally, Nonna's ultimate legacy: Each year, we gathered in her basement for Thanksgiving dinner. There would be lasagna, ravioli, meatballs, sausage, and salad, followed by turkey, cranberry sauce, stuffing, potatoes and vegetables. Nonna and her daughters prepared everything. These were special gatherings that began in the 1950s with 30-35 in attendance. There were two tables, one for the adults and one for the cousins. I longed to be at the adult table. When I finally got "promoted" in 1966, I felt like an adult until I realized it was a lot more fun at the other table, so I demoted myself!

That gathering continues today except it happens every other year and between 120 and 130 people attend. Many of that first gathering have passed away. This big number is mostly family, but keeping with Nonna's tradition, anyone who is alone for Thanksgiving can be included. Grace before dinner always includes a brief story about Nonna so that those who never knew her are at least aware of her impact and significance.

Mike DeGiorgi
Moneta, VA

CHAPTER VI

Meme Perris and
Helene, her daughter

Meme Mailhac
and family

Madeleine Perris, born Madeleine Gironce

Born: 1889 – Died: 1979

Maternal Grandmother

Meme Perris

My maternal grandmother was Madeleine Perris, born Madeleine Gironce. When my brothers and I spoke about her, we would call her "Meme Perris." She was born in Paris.

She was rather short and a little plump. She was pretty with a big braid of hair twisted around her head. When I was about five years of age, whenever my younger brother got an epidemic before me, I was "sent to my maternal parents" in order to keep me from catching the illness. Meme loved those visits, and each time, at the end of my stay, there was an inevitable crisis between my mother and her. She always found a reason to keep me for weeks or even months.

Once I saw her washing and combing her hair. I remember thinking that perhaps she never had her hair cut. It was dark brown and extremely long. I saw her sitting on a stool in front of the reclining mirror in her bedroom, and her hair fell from her shoulders onto the floor. She took a long time combing and braiding her hair and probably she did this exercise only once a week or so.

During those visits, she wanted to teach me to sing and to play the piano. With her, I learned a particularly lovely song from Brittany, and I played it on the piano. This was my first discovery of real music. I had had piano lessons before: my teacher was a man with enormous feet and hands. He wanted me to learn fast, and he had written numbers, '1 2 3, etc.' above the notes to help me remember which finger I was supposed to use. When Meme, looking at my music books, realized that I was playing numbers instead of notes, she was horrified and taught me everything the right way, or her way! I no longer sing or play the piano, unfortunately, but my intense need for music surely comes from my first steps with her. She herself had lived in an enchanted world of music since she was born. Her father was a well-known conductor in the French military, and she had studied singing and had played the piano throughout her youth. She missed that dimension in her life after she got married.

Meme Perris had help for some of the housework, but she was always the one going shopping for food every morning and preparing the meals.

She was picky about which shop to go to for the best ingredients. She was a superb – NO, rather a sublime cook! She could make a perfect soup with just a few leftovers. My grandfather had a rule: he never took seconds. So, she had to be creative. I wish I had some of her skills! Her cuisine, especially some of her desserts, brought tears to my eyes.

She was a passionate woman; her many hugs and kisses were long, ample and warm. Her marriage with Louis Perris had been an arranged marriage decided by her father and a friend of his. She had been a dutiful daughter, and she was a dutiful wife. I was her very first grandchild, she adored me, and I loved her immensely. When I married for love a young Asian man whom my parents did not welcome, she understood that love burning in me from day one, and she gave me her full support. Her unconditional love was infinitely precious to me at that moment in my life.

She was still alive when I graduated from the University of Poitiers, when we got married in 1969, and when we left France to go live in Thailand in 1970. A few years later, she even got to know her great-grandchildren. She was so happy we had had a girl and a boy!

When she died, we had left Thailand and settled in America. We had bought a house in Alexandria, Virginia. When no more of her long, loving letters came in the mail, I understood that the end was near. Meme Perris is forever present in me in the way I feel, the way I listen, the way I react to various events.

Jeanne Marsaud, born Jeanne Moreau

Born: 1890 – Died: 1965

Paternal Grandmother

Meme Mailhac

My paternal grandmother was Jeanne Marsaud, born Jeanne Moreau. We called her 'Meme' as well, and when we spoke about her, we called her 'Meme Mailhac', after the village where she and my grandfather had their farm.

Meme was lean and tall and had straight long auburn hair that she kept tied in a bun at the back of her head. I remember her wearing dresses and aprons. Sometimes she would tuck a big dish cloth on each side over the apron. She wiped her hands on the dishcloth, not on her apron. She ordered the aprons from a catalog, and they were made of a soft black cotton with tiny flower motifs in lighter colors – light blue, mauve or yellow. They had two seams in the front and marked her waist. She wore a new one every day. Interestingly, this type of apron is still made and sold today in France; it is still used by working women in the countryside. I remember that Meme's aprons had two little pockets. She would keep what I thought were "treasures" in those pockets: scissors, strings, safety pins, etc. If she lent one of those things to me, I had to return it to her as soon as I could and in perfect condition.

Mailhac-sur-Benaize is a village in the center of France. The Benaize is a little creek winding its way between the village and the bottom of my grandparents' farm. A main road crossed the village and went past the farmhouse to the top of the hill and beyond. Meme wore felt slippers over big socks and quickly slipped her feet into big wooden clogs when she needed to go outside and walk onto muddy parts of the farm. A huge courtyard and the barns, the cattle and most parts of the farm were behind the house, safe and protected behind big gates. I was afraid of the big animals and probably never ventured out there by myself. But chickens, ducks and geese were allowed to roam freely around the farm. It did happen, though, that a car rushed up onto our hill, did not stop for a foolish hen crossing the road at the wrong time and left it bloody where it had hit it (in french we would say : « her »). Meme immediately ran outside, picked up that ill-fated bird, mumbled some very angry words about the driver of the car and reorganized her day's tasks. Immediately the hen was put in a bucket of water, its feathers were plucked off one by one, then its body was prepared to be cooked. That evening there was delicious meat on the table. Meme's magic had transformed a heartbreak into something joyful to be shared by all.

She worked enormously. Even at a young age, I was fascinated by the multiplicity of tasks she could do. A lot were chores, probably, but each was tackled as something utterly important, having to be completed just now, later would be too late. I loved to help her inside or outside the house. I liked picking fruits or vegetables with her ; I helped set up the table ; I dried the washed dishes with a cloth, etc. I loved everything. I was sure that Meme herself loved everything she had to do at the farm. Little did I know that she was up at 4:00 am or 4:30 am and worked nonstop until she collapsed in bed around 9 or 10 in the evening!

At a young age Meme had fallen in love with a young man, Aristide Marsaud, and promptly married him. When WWI started, pregnant with my Uncle Aristide, she had to run the farm and to take care of her elderly in-laws as well. Her husband survived that war, fortunately, and my father, little Pierre, was born in 1920.

WWII was another terrible blow on that generation. My grandfather was a prisoner in Germany and came back a broken man. In 1950 Meme Mailhac was widowed. Her life brutally took a radically different turn. The farm had to be sold. Meme came to live with my parents who were both teaching and struggling to raise me plus my two, then three brothers. I will forever feel humbled by her selflessness. The workload in our house was different from her work on the farm, but it was substantial, too. My mother counted on her for everything. Meme was very resilient, always helpful, preparing us for school, repairing what needed to be fixed, cleaned, sewed back up. Meme Mailhac loved us equally—the four of us, boy or girl, the same. She was straightforward, frank, just.

When I was eleven, my family moved into a modern house. A brand-new television set immediately found its place in the living-room. Meme and my parents watched the news before dinner every day but every morning she picked up the newspaper and she read it thoroughly during the day. She was interested in what was going on in our region and France in general. When she discussed with my parents, she made intelligent comments. She was often insightful, even astute.

My mother received fashion magazines through the mail. She tried to follow the trends in fashion and to be up to date, modern, as « chic » as she could. Meme had always knitted for all of us. In the last years of her life she had a heart condition and was becoming very frail. But knitting had become a passion, and she seemed to still like the challenge of new styles and shapes. In the sixties, the Courreges style with boxy shapes and straight skirts above the knee, with lots of white and pastel colors, was all the rage. She made me quite a few Courreges-like outfits ! Being raised among boys I was a bit boyish myself. Meme sought to make me pretty. I was doing everything to make her proud.

How proud she was when I got my baccalaureat ! I was one year younger than my classmates.

Meme died while I was away in college. My mother had a career and I definitely wanted to follow a career path myself. But I have learned from Meme something vital : the realization that to be a woman is larger than having a career. It is to live with and for others and to be able to reinvent oneself many times during one's lifetime.

Catherine Habanananda
Washington, DC

CHAPTER VII

MooMoo, the late
Carole Sue Smith, with
Snickers, her labradoodle

Beautiful Carole

Carole Sue Smith

Date of Birth: September 4, 1941 – Date of Death: November 10, 2015

Paternal Grandmother

MooMoo

Carole Sue Smith's grandson, **Neil, is nine years old**. The questions provided to him emanated from the collector of these memoirs. Neil and his sister Isabel were asked these questions by their father, Carole Smith's son. They are in bold font and their answers are italicized.

What was the nickname for your grandmother?

MooMoo.

Do you have a favorite picture of MooMoo taken with you?

I do remember getting a picture. I remember doing one at the space museum. That one museum with the big plane inside of it. I think we took a few.

What did your grandmother look like?

She looked like you but a girl.

Anything else?

No.

Do you know where she lived?

Washington, DC. It was big and it had four floors and there were always pistachios on the table. She liked Hershey's kisses and there were Hershey Kisses by the Pistachios. She actually had five floors. She had a cool pond in the front yard. I think it's the front. The front yard is really cool because it has cool stuff in it. There was a TV above the kitchen – like on the corner of the kitchen, and there was a cool entrance into the house. She had beautiful rugs (while laughing) and she had lots of dog toys. There is a lot I can think about in the house. That's all I can remember because we haven't been there in like a year.

Do you remember her dogs?

Do you mean Snickers with the mustache and Jake with the beard? Snickers was not shy and Jake was timid. They were white and fluffy. They were small.

Did you spend Christmas with MooMoo?

Yes, I remember I got the Lego Coast Guard Boat and I remember eating a lot of Hershey's kisses and I remember being at the hotel and begging mommy and you to go to MooMoo's house. We stayed in a hotel nearby, I remember. There were cool ornaments. I remember we were sleeping upstairs and we thought we heard Santa because we heard reindeer steps on the roof.

Do you remember any toys she gave you that you still love to play with?

Buddy (Per Neil's father, Buddy is #2 stuffed animal. He sleeps with him every night and he totally associates Buddy with MooMoo). She gave me hot wheels that I put on my track a lot. She gave us a Huggle Pod. We play with the Huggle Pod and pretend it is a ship and we pretend we park at Islands. I think I remember MooMoo giving us a coloring book but she definitely gave us books.

Did she bake cookies or cakes for you?

Yeah. Didn't she do that dessert at Christmas? That thing she baked, cookies with mommy. I think like a long time ago she baked cookies.

Did she laugh a lot?

Yeah. Um. I remember when me and Isabel were playing and I heard you guys having a conversation and she was laughing. Her laugh kind of sounded like yours a bit.

Did you hear her sing?

I know she sang.

Do you remember something you did with MooMoo that you shared together and that will stay in your heart forever?

I remember when we were driving home from the airport and she had that computer thing so she could like talk. I thought that was really cool that there was a computer thing that reads what you type. She liked us a lot. She cared about you, Daddy. I remember seeing a picture of you with her when you were a kid. I remember she was pretty tall like you and she had that game where you bounce the ball on that little paddle thing.

Was she funny?

Yeah, her house kind of smells like chocolate.

After Neil's father said, "That's all."

Neil said, "That was a fun quiz."

Isabel is seven years old and Neil's sister. She was also asked the same questions from her father about her grandmother.

What was the nickname for your grandmother?

MooMoo.

Do you have a favorite picture of MooMoo taken with you?

No.

What did your grandmother look like?

She had black hair and she was so pretty and um, um, her eyes were like brownish blackish. Um. And that's it.

Anything else?

Nah. This is fun!

Do you know where she lived?

Washington, DC. Um. She has really long staircases, she has exercise machines upstairs, um, and when Annalise (her cousin), is over, we always do obstacle couches because she has a really long couch and we jump on the bed. And I sleep upstairs on the bed and she has a really comfortable blanket and she has two dogs named Jack, (Isabel's father states that sometimes she says 'Jack' and sometimes 'Jake') with a beard, and Snickers with a mustache, and we named them those. And she has a fish pond, three fish ponds, in the backyard and we always play in the backyard and she has a secret gate that leads to her neighbor's house. I've pretty much explained her whole house. And she lives in an alley kind of. Not like a homeless alley but like an alley. Are you going to send this to Leepa (Isabel's late grandmother's husband)?

Do you remember her dogs?

That's hard. They both have curly hair and we named them Snickers with a mustache and Jake with a beard. And I think Snickers probably likes Snickers. And um...they are really cute and they are small and one, I forgot which one it was, but one of the dogs ran away. Leepa had to run out and get him.

Did you spend Christmas with MooMoo?

Yes. So, um ... we did not get that many presents, actually we got a lot, our stockings were over filled and our tree was pretty and MooMoo gave us the rope ladder and the huggle pod. And, um...

also we got the bunny lights and it was really fun and in our stockings, I got smelly markers and a lot of other things. When we went home, we asked for a huge unicorn and a huge bear and when we went home they were under our Christmas tree. That's it.

Do you remember any toys or dolls she gave you that you still love to play with?

She didn't really give me toys or dolls. She gave me purses and necklaces. She also gave you some of her stuffed animals and then you gave us those stuffed animals. And she gave Neil a camera.

Did she bake cookies or cakes for you?

No I don't remember that. Actually, I think she made one cake and a few cookies. And she made really good cookies. And she made good lemonade. I think chocolate chip cookies.

Did she laugh a lot?

A cute laugh and that's it.

Did you hear her sing?

No.

Do you remember something you did with MooMoo that you shared together and will stay in your heart forever?

Her funeral. And when we were over at her house and when we were at the hotel and when me and Neil made up a phone number. I think it was 207 or 270. When we were doing that party with her and when we were going to that train museum with her but she didn't come.

Was she funny?

Yeah. She did good jokes. Oh, and MooMoo always had peppermints and she always had Snickers, not the dog Snickers, but the candy Snickers, on the coffee table.

Brandon Vogt
Colorado Springs, CO

CHAPTER VIII

Grandma with Danielle, her granddaughter

Photos from the past and the passage of time

Josephine (Jo) Guasto Belizzone

Date of Birth: March 1, 1935 – Date of Death: June 5, 2014

Maternal Grandmother

Grandma

My grandmother, who I called, 'Grandma,' was born in Brooklyn, New York, and she was one of six children. Her family was Italian, and we are Italian as well. Grandma did not speak Italian and both her parents were born here in the United States. She met my grandfather in Brooklyn, but when she graduated high school, she and her family moved to Long Island. When my grandparents were married in 1956, they moved to Manville, New Jersey. My grandmother's father was building houses in that town, so my grandparents bought one of them. They later moved to Bridgewater, New Jersey, and this is the home I remember. Many unforgettable memories were made there.

My grandparents had seven grandchildren, and I was the only granddaughter. I am the oldest and only girl, so all my cousins joked that I was the favorite. My grandmother and I had a special relationship when I was little that became even stronger as I grew up. I remember sleeping over my grandparents' home with or without my brother. She always made my birthdays very special. We would pick which mall we could go to, and she and I would go shopping. We would walk around the mall holding hands, and she and I had our special day. Another thing that we always did around Christmas time was when we went into New York City. I remember going to my first Broadway show with her when I was 13 years old. It was an amazing experience, and we even ate dinner at a restaurant called The Fashion Café. She and my grandfather were always in New York City going to shows and theaters, so she knew her way around The Big Apple. She would tell me stories of when she was younger and how she and her siblings would take public transportation all by themselves at such a young age. It sure was a different time back then.

Every Christmas we would go to New York City to see the Christmas Spectacular. Sometimes we would drive, and other times we took the train. We would always go out to dinner, walk around Rockefeller Center and take a look at the stores on Fifth Avenue. One year we did take two of my male cousins, but after that, we decided to keep our trip to "just us girls." When my grandmother was healthy and doing well, we would go every year. The last year we went I told her that I wanted to take her to the show and buy the tickets since she had done so much for me for so many years. My grandmother developed some breathing issues and was now on oxygen. Getting in and out of the city was then too much for her, and she watched the tree lighting on television, as I still do now. These memories are still very vivid and very special to me.

My grandmother always wanted to be a great-grandmother to a granddaughter. My husband and I dated four years, and she would say, "When are you going to get engaged?" My grandmother offered me her diamond, and I said to her, "You need to talk to Ed (who was my boyfriend), and you tell him." She never held back from anything. He was over her house doing work one day, and she said she would love to offer my diamond. He said, "When I am ready to propose, I will call you and come get it, transfer it to a new setting, and then I will bring it back to you." When he was ready, he spoke to my dad, went to my grandmother and watched the jeweler transfer the diamond to the new setting. I have my grandmother's diamond in my engagement ring, and she had her ring re-set with a stone from my grandfather's wedding band. At my wedding, a beautiful photo was taken of my hand and my grandmother's hand with our rings on.

My grandmother was not that tall – average height. She had dark hair, and she was classy. She always looked good with makeup and dressed to a 'T', always had on her nice jewelry, and her nails were always done. She was very honest, spoke her mind, and never held anything back. She would give me her honest opinion, and sometimes she would say things people did not want to hear. She was very family oriented – always had the family over at Christmas, at her house. My cousins and I have so many good memories of my grandparents, the house they lived in, the built-in bar and chairs that turned. My grandpa was always behind the bar. My grandma liked vodka on the rocks with an olive. I will always remember the way they wrapped the gigantic pile of Christmas presents. They stacked them up very high – the last one on top was an ornament every year and wrapped in a nice bow. Every year when we decorate our Christmas tree, I am reminded of the wonderful memories because of all the special ornaments I received from my grandparents over the years. Each of us seven grandchildren had their own stack of Christmas gifts! During these holidays, my grandfather sat at the head of the table and my grandmother to the right. I sat in between the two of them!

Grandma was always very active and on the go. She also had lots of friends as well. My mom and my grandma were very close. My grandparents traveled everywhere and had a group of friends who they traveled with. They were called 'The Pocono Eight' – going on cruises, vacations, and different places together. When my grandmother was sick, she said, "Your grandfather and I had a beautiful life together." They loved each other so much – it was always so nice to see them together. My grandfather passed away at 81. A few years back, he started having symptoms of Alzheimer's disease. It was rough for Grandma to take care of him. He went to a nursing home, and my grandmother always said, "Your grandfather is going to outlive me – he is as healthy as a horse – if I could take his health and he my mind, we would be a perfect person."

One day my mom and I went over to see Grandma. I was ten weeks pregnant, and we thought that maybe we should tell Grandma, as she needed to be cheered up. She was so excited – we showed her the ultrasound picture – she always wanted a great-granddaughter. The doctor does a blood test to check for various genetic disorders, and the test can also tell the sex of our baby. When the doctor called with the results, we asked him to put the sex of the baby in a sealed envelope because we were going to have a small 'gender reveal party.' We took the envelope revealing the sex to the bakery. They baked a cake, and on the inside, they would make the icing pink for a girl or blue for a boy. We had the party, and my husband and I did not know the sex either. We invited the immediate family and my best friend. We had pizza and cut the cake. Everyone wanted to have dessert first because they were so excited, but we ate pizza and then cut the cake. I said to my grandmother, "What do you think I am having?" My grandmother said, "I think a boy." I said to her, "You always said you wanted a great- granddaughter." She said, "I don't want to jinx it." When we cut the cake and pulled the cake cutter out, there was pink icing!

My grandma was so happy. At the end of May 2015, she started not feeling well and unfortunately, went into the hospital. She was looking forward to the birth of my daughter and would always say that she just wanted to hold the baby. I told my grandmother that I will tell my daughter stories about her and I will show her photos. My grandma wanted to buy the crib for me, and she did. My mom asked my grandma when she was in the hospital if she still wanted the crib to be from her and of course, she said 'yes.' There was money put aside for the crib.

When grandma was in the hospital, there were people there a lot: my mom, dad, aunt, uncle, her nieces, nephews and grandchildren. I wanted to get some alone time with her. I went and saw her a lot over a few days. I remember there was one point when we were alone, and she said she was ready to go – and I said, "I am not ready to let you go." I felt so bad for her as she was in this position – how do you accept it? We had a name picked out for my daughter, and I told grandma, "I want to name her after you." Grandma responded, "Don't you dare do that – I have disliked my name my whole life… don't do that to her." So we told my grandmother the name we chose, Marisa, and she absolutely loved it.

The day before my grandmother passed away, I had taken off from work to be at her house. Our immediate family was there, and it was nice to be all together. I know my grandma felt all of the love. My mom and aunts slept over that night. That morning my mom told me to go to work; if anything happened, they would call me. As I was doing my make-up, I just didn't feel right not being by my grandmother's side. I decided to take a half-day and leave work at 11:30 am. When I got to her house, I was able to hold her hand, kiss her, and tell her how much I loved her. My mom, her sister and their great aunt, and my cousin were there by her side. Grandma died at home with hospice care that day and we were all there for her. I was there when she passed away, and I am so glad that I was able to take the time off and be with her.

My grandmother collected a lot of Llladro that she kept in her cabinet. When she passed away, my mom and my aunt got some pieces. One day my mom and dad came over with a huge box – a beautiful Lladro angel and a little girl next to her. It was so beautiful. We wanted to put it in my daughter's room, but it did not fit on her hutch so now we have it in our living room. One day we will put it in my daughter's room or our dining room. We have my grandparents' dining room set so it would also look great in the china cabinet.

When I think of my grandma, I feel many emotions because I miss her so much. However, I feel blessed and thankful for the wonderful memories I keep close to my heart every day. I know that she is watching over my daughter and all of us, so that gives me comfort.

My grandma taught me so much about life, love and family. I will continue to honor the memories I have of her and tell my daughter about her great-grandma who loved her very much before she was even born.

One thing my grandma always said to me when something happened was, "Well, that chapter has closed, and a new one has started." Even though I have started this chapter of my life without Grandma's physical presence, I know she is close at heart, and I will always love her.

Danielle Amodeo Caulfield
Bridgewater, New Jersey

CHAPTER IX

Grandmother Annette

Minnie Annette Hill Wilkins

Date of Birth: December 5, 1889 – Date of Death: June 27, 1974

Maternal Grandmother

Grandmother Annette

When I think of my maternal grandmother, many beautiful things come to mind. My grandmother's name was: Minnie Annette Hill Wilkins, and my four brothers and I called her Annette. It was only much later in life that I discovered she did not like to be called Annette by her grandchildren. I wish she had told me. I would have respectfully called her 'Grandmother' or whatever name she would have preferred. My little brothers called her 'Grandma.' She was born in a small southern town in Carrolton, Mississippi, in the Northern Delta area and had only one brother, Eugene Hill. Her mother, Minnie Hill, died at age 26 from typhoid fever. It always made me sad that she grew up never knowing her beautiful young mother. Consequently, she and Uncle Gene never once had a fuss about anything, and he was always so sweet to her.

My memory of her was that she was physically short and round with small brown eyes that gazed directly into yours. She had excellent eyesight – even able to notice pimples on my face as a teenager and let me know when they had cleared up. I remember one day when she commented how much better my skin looked. Her hair was dark brown, short and naturally curly. She told me when she was a young teenager she could sit on her hair and would braid it up very stylishly. I have a beautiful picture on my dresser of her braided hair at age seventeen. She was even-tempered, a great speller and loved to be challenged to spell any word. She spoke perfect grammatical English and won several awards in elocution.

My grandmother was a true Southern belle in every sense of the word. She would always dress well before leaving her home to go anywhere and showed me how to wear perfume on my wrists, under my ears and with just a touch of it under my nose so I could smell it too! She loved to entertain and gave fabulous parties using all her fineries to entertain her guests. She was a wonderful cook and made her own homemade pocket rolls with yummy melted butter inside the folded over pockets. This was a tradition she passed down to my mother and on to some of my brothers. Michael, my third brother, has always made the best, just like hers! I have yet to make her rolls but I will one day! Every Thanksgiving she served pickled peaches in a crystal compote and made her special ambrosia with the perfect combination of her delicious coconut cake for everyone. This was a favorite tradition mother always did, and I always continue to serve each year.

My grandmother was always delightful to be around. How I love to remember those summer evenings when my cousins, neighbors and close friends would come over for some iced tea and a visit with Miss Annette and Mr. Ches (called Chesley), my granddaddy (their affectionate names). Mama, the boys and I would all sit in the living room with the adults, listening to the stories they would tell and the conversations that kids typically weren't interested in but knew to be polite and respectful around. To the side of their living room was the music room with a baby grand piano and Hammond organ. Annette and Papa (Pah Pah) loved to be entertained with both instruments, and my mother would always play her amazing 30s ragtime-style renditions that gave the evening a fun, delightful atmosphere. I often remember my grandparents asking me to sing. My little brother, Michael, would play the piano with his classical and original jazz flair, too. Sometimes our cousin, Olivia, would join in and play her own piano arrangements. Our Uncle Chesley also had a pretty voice and loved to sing hymns. My father also played classical and only had one year of training. Needless to say, we were a pretty musical family.

There are still precious memories that will always stay with me. I remember when we would sit outside on the front porch, and I would nurse my bottle, snuggled up in my grandmother's lap. She rocked me, and we looked up at the stars and waited for the train to come by. I'd give anything to go back then and feel the security of her holding me in her lap with arms around me on those warm summer nights in Duck Hill as a little toddler. Money can't buy moments like these. They are gifts that come from a grandparent's tender heart.

We would love for our grandmother to come visit us at our home in Charleston, Mississippi, about 45 miles north of Duck Hill where she and Papa lived. She had her own genteel manner about her when she would greet my friends at the front door, welcoming them and proudly stating, *"Won't you come in? I am Dorothy Jeanne's grandmother."* Even when she signed her letters to me, she would always sign with her full name, *"Your loving grandmother, Annette Hill Wilkins."* It was a formal signature but so endearing.

It's hard to believe, but back in the late 1950s, my grandmother still wore a corset. I remember Pah Pah lacing it for her even up into the 1960s. Then as styles became more modern, she decided to let it go and finally be relaxed with more casual attire. I don't even remember her wearing black slacks, but she did wear sundresses. When my mother and my Aunt Jean were little girls, she sewed beautifully, and she made all their little dresses out of organza with lovely lace collars and satin bows. I have a picture of my mother in one of those dresses holding her doll at age five. How I love that picture.

Grandmother Annette was very organized and so very generous. In July she would start collecting Christmas gifts for everyone, both for family and for friends. She would start picking things out with so many of us in mind and laid them out with each person's name tagged to each gift on her guest bed. She thought of everyone.

When I was a little girl, I visited my grandmother a lot. My grandfather was Chairman of the Board of the Duck Hill Bank there in Duck Hill, where Mother, Dorothy Anderson Wilkins, and my Aunt Mary Jeanne and Uncle Chesley were born. She and Pah Pah only lived one block from the bank, and they would come home for lunch to a delicious homemade cooked meal by Peg, their housekeeper. Peg was also known as "Big Annie" and worked for them faithfully for fifty years. Peg and Annette would greet us kids with great bear hugs full of love when we came for our summer visits. They always made the most wonderful meals for us, serving at least six vegetables on our plates from their garden with homemade corn bread and the best iced tea in the whole wide world that only Peg could make. How could I forget her special caramel cake? Oh, so delicious! Even now, I can still taste it all in my mind. I sat next to Pah Pah, and he taught me to love to eat okra, which reminds me of him every time I eat it.

I was a bit of a naughty little girl because I used to get into my grandmother's makeup. I can hear her now scolding me, *"Dorothy Jeanne, get out of my rouge."* She always knew what I was up to. I think she had eyes in the back of her head! I would see her put on her makeup in front of her vanity and say, *"Dorothy, would you like to go downstairs and visit Ms. Rob today and have some iced tea?"* I said, *"Yes, ma'am,"* and she would cut my bangs and even them out, get out the rouge and put a little on my cheeks – no lipstick. She would then find a fresh little sundress for me and make sure it was pressed and that it looked nice on me. We would go into her bottom chest of drawers, and I would have the choice of choosing a beautiful lace handkerchief and one of her gorgeous fans. She had so many, and they were all so lovely. What a treat they were for me! It was hard for me to choose. After we were dressed, she found her umbrella, and we walked underneath to keep the sun off of our faces. My grandmother warned me as a child never to let the sun shine on my face so that I would have a pretty complexion. I have always kept this as a rule even to this day. She always had cream to moisten her skin, lotion for her hands and always cleaned and polished her diamond rings. These are rituals I still do to this day which always remind me of her.

When I was nineteen and in my second year at Stephens College in Columbia, Missouri, I had an epiphany that suddenly came to me out of the blue one day. I realized how I had taken my grandmother for granted as a child and teenager after all of her unconditional love for me throughout my life. I then decided to sit down and write her a loving letter and told her how sorry I was that I did not tell her how much I loved her and how much she meant to me. I asked her to please forgive me. When I saw her in person, she reassuringly told me that she knew I loved her, and we had a sweet, loving embrace that let me know all was well.

In summary, I want to say that I was exceedingly blessed to be the granddaughter of Minnie Annette Hill Wilkins. I loved her with all my heart, and I still do. My grandmother Annette had the highest level of integrity, and I have to say that I never saw a flaw in her character. She was a virtuous woman with a strong faith in God who was loved and admired by everyone who knew her, especially my grandfather who worshiped the ground she walked on. It is hard to live up to her because she has always been on a pedestal to me, but deep inside, I aspire to be like her. I long for the day when she greets me at the gate in heaven and says, *"Welcome home, Dorothy Jeanne. It's me, your loving grandmother, Annette Hill Wilkins"* and we embrace with a great big hug!

Jeanne Sheffield Estrada
Washington, D.C.

CHAPTER X

Grandma with grandson, Ryan

Mary Caruso

Maria Salvatrice Pelliccione (Maiden Name)
Date of Birth: March 5, 1924. Not deceased.
Maternal Grandmother
Grandma

We all called my maternal grandmother 'grandma.' She was born in Lawrence, Massachusetts, in Lawrence Hospital. When I was born I lived there, in her house, with my mom and grandparents as my dad was in the military and stationed in Korea. Grandma helped raise me with my mom for the first year of my life, in her home. The town of Lawrence was called 'Immigrant City' as there were more people of all different backgrounds than anywhere else in the country.

I had a special connection with my grandmother. She always nurtured me, artistically. There was something creative and artistic about her. My grandfather built a beach house on Plum Island which is approximately a 25-minute drive from Lawrence, on the Northern Coast of Massachusetts.

Grandma was a seamstress by trade and worked for 40 years at Grieco Brothers in Lawrence Massachusetts. Most of the women who worked there were Italian. They recruited a few Syrians, Armenians and eventually Puerto Rican young women. Grandma spoke Sicilian but also learned a good deal of Spanish. She taught me some Spanish and Sicilian. Her parents were too poor in Italy to learn proper Italian, and therefore she never learned it as well.

She always used to tell me that someone from Grieco Brothers would go to New York and wait for the boat for immigrants and pull off the Italians – to bring them to Lawrence as they were good sewers. She worked eight hours a day, sewing, and during her lunch break she would use leftover materials to make clothes for my mom and my mom's sister. Grandma always made clothes for talent shows, clothes for pets and even stuffed animals. She would learn very quickly and even braided rugs. She was curious which led her to look up information in books on: how to knit sweaters, to crochet, braid materials, etc. All her clothing was homemade. She was constantly sewing. When she lived at the beach on Plum Island, she would make crafts by taking shells and driftwood and then making ashtrays. She would paint things, color and glue as well. She was always very creative. Even when I was very little, I always felt we had a special connection – she could identify the artistic sensibilities that I had and we connected with that. I felt I could tell her anything.

My grandmother had three brothers and was the oldest child. She wanted to go into the WAVES which was the female version of the Navy, but her father got angry and refused as he did not want a girl to go into the military. When my grandmother was young, in her late teens, she was sent to the Bronx for a year and ended up taking singing lessons.

My grandfather died when I was 17. This was in 1989. He died, we went to his funeral, and later that year, my grandmother joined a performance group – called Comedy Masque Review and she was with them for 25 years. She performed with them until she was 90! When she started, she was the youngest in the group and they performed shows in retirement homes, boat cruises, including places in New Hampshire. They also performed at Winnekinne Castle, which is a little castle that was used as an event space.

When my grandfather died, she began to live. I think of my grandma as a kind of 'Sicilian Edith Bunker.' My grandmother was passive and introverted in many ways but she lived for this performance group. Some of my favorite memories are: "Ryan, come here, I have to play Ruth Buzzi, and I have to go with this number and with this guy -- he will flirt with me." She would also make costumes for these performances. She would add, "I don't know how you memorize" and I would say, "You will enjoy memorizing, you will love it." She always loved to sing. I went to see one of her performances in a church and it was cute. My mom would say grandma was not emotional, but grandma would say that she was not sentimental. Grandma would state, "Oh, these elderly people, Ryan, they love to come to rehearsals but if they don't show, call the family, and if someone does not show up, they must be dead."

She always had a self-portrait on her wall when she was in her early twenties. She was taller than my mother - perhaps 5'3" or 5'4". When she was growing up, she was taller than *her* mother. She was tall and elegant looking. For someone who was very much on the shy, stoic side, I saw pictures of her in a bikini in a photo album. She had a great figure. "Oh, I would get looks from all the men as you were not supposed to wear them and show your midsection."

She was a great cook yet my grandfather was a better cook. He loved to make meatballs and lived for food which eventually killed him. When he was dying and in the hospital, we went up to Massachusetts. He could not speak, as he was ridden with cancer and diabetes. We were gathered around the bed, and Grandma was talking about the 'mercy meal.' She said, "I should go cook and make the sauce…" She was talking about the funeral in front of him. "If people are coming over, I have to cook." My grandfather started to say something, and we all gathered around, and my uncle was there. Grandma said, "Fred, what are you trying to tell us?" He responded, "Make the sauce." Grandma started to laugh – only a dying Italian would say this – "The food is what is killing you." We all laughed and he passed away that night.

In her marriage, Grandma was very passive and almost shy so she broke convention in many ways. She was a product of her time. About ten years ago I was visiting and in the car with her. She liked to go to the Mall to walk around. I asked her when she was growing up, how old did she think she would end up being when she died. She said, "I never thought about being old - I just wanted my two children to get married -- then I could die." She had two daughters seven years apart.

Grandma was aloof, stoic and unemotional. Most Italian women are not perceived that way. I never saw her cry. Her brothers spoke to my mom about Grandma's brothers about how poor they were. Grandma said, "We were poor and did not know it." She was not demonstrative about emotions. She said she did not want to address that she was poor – one girl with three younger brothers. Grandma was too proud to address how poor they were.

Grandma is alive and at 92 in great health. She goes up and down stairs and lives with my aunt and her daughter. She misses the dogs that they used to have and loved it when I brought my dog to visit. My cousin and her husband live next door. She still does yard work and has a little garden. She also graveled the driveway.

Grandma was always lean and walked a lot. She had her vegetables and ate really well. In the last year she has gained a little weight. Although she seemed passive in many ways, we went to a wedding this past November, and she did not mind tearing up the dance floor at her granddaughter's wedding. One memory I have is that when we went to the beach, she would say, "Kids, go pick periwinkles off the rocks; whatever you gather from the ocean, will be good." She would then sauté them in garlic and butter, and they were delicious.

Grandma and I did have a strong connection in many ways. We even have similar eyes – light brown. Everyone else in the family has dark eyes.

Through these eyes, we saw the world in a very similar way, artistically. As an adult, I do see how she nurtured me creatively and I think I still carry that impression with me. I am an actor today, and Grandma is thrilled and impressed that I use my creativity that was indeed inspired by her. She also inspired my mom in the same way as my mom was involved in doing a lot of crafts, singing and playing the guitar.

Ryan Duncan
New York, NY

CHAPTER XI

Chapitre VI
Pour Isabelle,
avec beaucoup
d'amour.

Catherine

Grandma Grace

Grandma Nita

Grace Francis Weaver

Date of Birth: 1892 – Date of Death: 1989
Maternal Grandmother
Grandma Grace

My first memory of Grandma Grace was in 1959 when she arrived from Japan in a Constellation prop plane with three tails. She was born and lived in Japan. I was about four years old and was very impressed by this well-dressed, gracious, proper woman. She came to visit my mother, her other daughter and son, and her new grandchildren who were here in the United States. I don't remember much about that visit; I think she brought us some Japanese coloring books and crayons that looked and smelled foreign but somehow exotic.

After my grandfather died in Kobe, Japan, in 1959, she moved to the United States three years later to a beautiful apartment in San Francisco on top of Pacific Heights with a view of the Golden Gate Bridge. Her apartment, like her, was very 'proper' with a décor very much done in the British style with fine porcelain and furniture. The apartment, like her, was very elegant but not too pretentious.

Grandma Grace was extremely well dressed. She always wore hose, heels, and with a medium-length string of blue pearls, which matched her white, relatively medium-short, curled hair. For the rest of her life, she continued to wear her large diamond wedding ring, a ring that my wife proudly wears today as her wedding ring.

Grandma Grace and her only sister were born in Japan, and their mother died when they were three or four years old. I do not know anything about her father except that he was very wealthy and owned a large shipyard in Kobe. He re-married, and his new wife did not like the girls, and they were sent to a boarding school in England. Grandma Grace and her sister Lillian lived in England, at a boarding school, until she was 18 years old. After she graduated, she moved back to Japan, which was always a curious mystery for me. When I was seven years old, I asked her why she moved back to Japan, and she replied in a very British voice, "I moved to Japan because that was my home." Being a Brit and living in England all that time, this never made any sense to me.

She spoke fluent Japanese and English, and in her early twenties, married a man in Japan who was half Italian and half Japanese. My Grandfather

Louis was in the import/export business from Genoa, Italy, and his family had been there since the 1800s. He was a very wealthy man, and they had a huge mansion in Yokahama, which was destroyed in a major earthquake in 1929.

Grandma Grace had a very dry sense of humor and was very quiet and reserved. Her favorite activity was going to the library and reading novels. Watching her read was viewing a woman in her own world, but she was also very cultured and loved art. She would never volunteer information about herself unless I asked her. She never once said, "I love you." Instead, we would say, "I love you" and she would say, with a British accent, "I know." She never told my mother that she loved her either. She was very British and very controlled, and I never saw her get mad; she had a real stiff upper lip.

My most impressionable memory of her was when she took me to a beautiful museum in San Francisco. My mother had dressed me in a little sports coat and tie, and I took the bus over to her house and then we both took a bus to get there. I remember her saying when she saw me, "One must always look and act like a proper gentleman." This was one of the most influential things that affected my entire behavior and attitude for the rest of my life. To this day when I go out in public professionally, I always wear a tie, cufflinks and a jacket and even want my socks to match properly!

Anita Valero

Date of Birth: 1891 – Date of Death: 1990

Paternal grandmother

Grandma Nita

Grandma Nita lived in Yettem, a little town in the San Joaquin Valley of California, nestled near the Sierra Nevada foothills. She was born in Mexico, in Zacatecas, to a large family. Her father was a professor at a university, and her grandfather came from Spain. Both her father and grandfather were also wealthy, but I never knew how or why. He married his daughter off to a man who was a mayor of a very little town when she was very young. For economic reasons, they came to the United States illegally in 1917.

As a result of improvement in Mexico, they went back, but then returned again, legally, in the early 1920s. Some of my aunts and uncles were born in Mexico and some in the United States, but around the time of the Depression, my grandfather went back to Mexico and abandoned her and his family.

Grandma Nita lived with her brother along with his family and her children. They were very poor and worked as farm laborers in the fields from a very young age. Her brother was rather mean to her, and he had them live in a two-room house on his ranch with a dirt floor.

My grandmother only had a 3rd-grade education and did not speak English. She raised seven children, three girls and four boys, and she did not re-marry until her three daughters were adults because she was concerned about the safety of her daughters. She married a man named Carmen Tafoya in 1948 or 1949. He was technically my step-grandfather, but to me, he was always my grandfather – the only one I ever knew.

They are a great American success story. My grandfather and Grandma Nita picked in the fields as laborers for 30 years. Unlike their peers who wasted their money on beer and cheap toys, they individually saved their money, and when they got married, they bought a one-acre home in Yettem. He built a one-room country store, and the store was very successful. They ended up purchasing 40 acres of land behind them, and my grandfather farmed that land. They both did not speak English until 1967.

I spent one month every summer with my grandparents starting when I was a little boy up until I was in my senior year of high school. The thing about my grandmother that impressed me the most was that she and my grandfather were always working diligently at everything they did. Grandpa made sure the store was always neat, clean, and orderly with all the cans lined up on the shelves, and Grandma Nita kept detailed books on the finances.

Although she was not educated, she was very smart. There was a plan to build a highway through the nearby town of Visalia, and instead of letting the state tear down the houses in the way, she got the idea of buying the houses, having them moved to their property, and renting them out to farm workers. From this simple idea, they generated a significant income, and between the store, the farm, and the rentals, and living frugally, they ended up dying as multi-millionaires!

They did not look as if they had money. Grandma Nita wore very simple work clothes and always wore a large cotton apron with big pockets. Her only adornments were some very large, Aztec-like gold earrings. Grandpa always wore a work shirt, work pants and a straw hat.

Grandma Nita was a fabulous cook! She made what could best be described as "Mexican-country" style food that is both very simple but extremely tasty. She made corn tortillas by growing the corn, drying it, grinding it to mesa, and then making the tortillas! She would grind up chilies by hand and stir all her pots with a porcelain metal spoon that I have inherited. Her food was beyond anything you could get in a restaurant.

The other interesting thing about them was that, unlike both my parents, they were Republicans. My grandparents were long-time Reagan supporters – both when Reagan was Governor and later when he ran for President. They were such huge donors toward his campaigns that they were invited to his inauguration. Not being elegant like my British grandmother, they just taped the invitation up on the wall! They earned everything they did and worked for during their lives. I learned from them, and they always said to me in Spanish, "Work hard – save your money."

My grandmother Nita was perhaps my biggest inspiration – the way she lived by fighting many odds, still coming through and finally, making it to the top. I will never forget her determination and strength. She will always remain the motivating factor in my life.

One very hot summer day we were walking back from the store across a dusty road, and she stopped right in the middle and said, "Your father says you are a very smart boy. I think so too. I think one day you are going to be a very wealthy man." That one statement profoundly stuck in my mind like a prophecy and was the catalyst that inspired me to be the success I am today.

Wayne Estrada
San Francisco, CA

CHAPTER XII

Nana, My Grandmother Rose

Rose A. Klein Friedenberg

Date of Birth: June 1, 1893 – Date of Death: February 6, 1976

Maternal Grandmother

Nana

My Grandmother Rose

My Nana, that's what we nine grandchildren called her, was a warm loving woman with a sharp wit and tongue: 99 percent of what she said was out of love; the other 1 percent made us laugh. Nana would have been about 120 years old in 2014, had she lived, and Jewish people say "until 120" meaning may she live till then, but I'd like to think a little bit of her lives in all of us. Nana married young and not for love although the marriage produced four children in quick succession: three girls and then a boy. Grandpa was unimpressed with the last birth; even a son didn't warm him the way Nana was innately.

Nana was curious which lead her to study anything and everything from a foreign language to political subjects at the New School in New York even into her eighties. She also worked in the family real estate business in New York City almost to the end of her life because she enjoyed it. She liked to keep busy; she enjoyed entertaining and cooking for family and her many friends. She was welcoming, always at her door, with open arms and a funny smile, her lips closed. When the door opened of her New York apartment, one could smell the 'hank of hair piece of bone' absolute deliciousness of her cooking. No recipes, just perfection. She also was very beautiful. Nana was also honored many times for her affiliation to Hadassah and the Jewish Museum in New York. She kept a kosher home with Grandpa although until his death they had owned and lived in forty different homes, one for each year of marriage.

As a teenager, Nana supported her mother after the older children left home which meant leaving school and working as a secretary. She married at 21, had the children and entered into a fruitful, busy, entertaining-filled life with four very different children, all of whom adored her. She was accepting of differences, accepting of most people and disparaged about one percent with good humor.

Nana suffered greatly through enormous and critical illnesses, the death of two of her daughters, two sons-in-law as well as her husband, my grandpa, when she was still quite young. Yet still she had the tenacity to cling to life by extending herself to others and, to her credit, enjoying her own life but being selfless and not selfish.

Although dogs frightened her, Nana always welcomed my dachshund into her home. We didn't see each often because we were separated by miles, but she was there for me. She was THERE for me. My greatest regret reflects on me: I was unable to face her death as she lay in the hospital surrounded by many other family members. Being the wonderful, gentle, funny, sweet, self-educated, much appreciated human being she was, I do not doubt for a moment this angel in heaven knows how much I love(d) her.

Carol R. Adler
Cambridge, MA

CHAPTER XIII

Grandmom and also called Grandmother

Margaret Lucille King Spillane

Date of Birth: March 8, 1911 – Date of Death: November 26, 1994

Maternal Grandmother

Grandmom /Grandmother

My name is Liz Beegle. My grandmother's name was Margaret Lucille King Spillane. She was born in 1911 and died at age 83, the Saturday after Thanksgiving, 1994, my freshman year in college.

She was my maternal grandmother, and we called her "Grandmom" or "Grandmother." My mom and her siblings called their mother "Mama," and it always sounded full of love when I heard them refer to their mother in this way.

Grandmother was an Irish Catholic woman from the Scranton, Pennsylvania, area. She and her husband, James Spillane, a plumber, moved to Washington, DC, for work during World War II. They ultimately ended up in the Brookland neighborhood of DC and raised eight children in a small duplex next to the Divine Word Seminary, down the street from the Franciscan Monastery and a few blocks from the National Shrine of the Immaculate Conception and the Catholic University of America.

My grandmother always struck me as a gentle woman. She worked as the secretary to the English Department at Catholic University. The family story is that the department needed to replace her with several employees at her retirement because she was so efficient in her role. Although she did not graduate from high school, but rather did a secretarial course, she was always a reader, and my mom often impressed upon us the rigor of her early education. The details of her life all came to me from my mother and other family members because my grandmother's memory was deteriorating by the time I was aware of her. She called my younger sister and me the "little girls," not remembering our names. However, I have children's books and cards dedicated in her beautiful script "To Elizabeth Ann."

My early memories of my grandmother are the many Sunday dinners and family birthday parties we had at her house in Brookland. We loved to play in her long back yard with a hammock between two large maples, borders of daylilies and lilies of the valley. She often sat in her front room with stacks of periodicals and newspapers piled neatly near the couch.

As her memory declined, my uncle, who lived with her, would bring her out to our house in the suburbs for the weekends. He went out of town to sell his photos at art shows. My sister and I often spent Sunday evenings with her while my parents were out. She didn't speak much by that time, but was pleasant when spoken to and very docile. When I was on my own with my grandmother, I felt it difficult to connect with this elderly woman who did not remember many things. It was much easier to understand her in the context of her children, my aunts and uncles, surrounding her, reminding her of the things she liked or was interested in. One thing we could share was reciting prayers together. Her faith played a central role in her life, and her memory clung on to the words to prayers and religious customs long after she had forgotten my name or knew how to dress herself without prompting. It was beautiful to see her reverently bless herself with the sign of the Cross before we said a Rosary together or recited Grace before meals.

She finally needed to move into the secure dementia unit at The Washington Home. For a short time, I went to high school in Northwest DC and could walk over to visit with her in the afternoon. I think my sister and I treasured this time because we were older and realized our grandmother's life was ending. When we watched her on Sunday nights when we were younger, it seemed to be more of a burden, making sure she was okay and got to bed safely. Now, a little more mature ourselves and without the responsibility of keeping her safe, we tried to reach out and connect with whatever part of her personality remained accessible. Here again, the shared heritage of prayers helped us engage in something meaningful with our grandmother.

My parents and my sisters and I visited my grandmother in the nursing home on Thanksgiving. She died in her sleep that Friday night. At her funeral Mass, when the family was processing out of the church following the casket, I burst into tears. This shocked me. I hadn't thought I knew my grandmother, so how could I mourn her with tears? My Aunt Sheila enveloped me in a hug and told me it was okay. This aunt had been a loving and generous daughter to her mother in her declining years, traveling back from California to visit with her often, always speaking in such a gentle manner to my grandmother, supporting her dignity as a fellow human being and as a beloved mother. Her assurance that I loved my grandmother and could cry at her funeral has helped me feel connected to my grandmother to this day. Now, I enjoy talking to my mother and learning more about the woman who was my grandmother.

Elizabeth Beegle
Silver Spring, MD

CHAPTER XIV

Grandma Schmidt

Henrietta Wilhemina Christina Miller Schmidt

Date of Birth: 1880 – Date of Death: 1966

Maternal Grandmother

Grandma Schmidt

My grandmother was the last born in a family of five boys and two girls in Green Island, Iowa, to Claus and Henrietta Schneider Miller, a prosperous farming family who immigrated to the Midwest from central Germany in the mid-1800s. The Millers, as did many other immigrants, stopped and settled where they found a landscape that reminded them of their homeland, which for them was the green, rolling hills and rich farmland of Eastern Iowa, along the banks of the Mississippi River.

Most of the Miller and Schneider descendants stayed within a 100-mile radius of where they grew up. Family reunions were de rigueur and traditions and kinship were passed along to the next generation. It is within this framework of stability, continuity and close family associations that Henrietta Miller married George Schmidt with whom she had a son and two daughters, the youngest of whom was my mother, Lucinda. George and "Etta" owned a successful farm near Preston, Iowa, on which they grew grain and corn, butchered and smoked beef and pork, raised chickens and ducks, tended a huge garden and orchard from which fruits and vegetables were canned and stored for use during the long, severe Midwest winters.

The farmhouse and farm were sold shortly after I was born, and the Schmidts moved to a big, white, corner house in Preston. After Grandpa Schmidt died in 1949, I began to spend summers with Grandma Schmidt in that white house on the corner. She was 69, and I was only seven, yet we were a perfect match. She introduced me to a love of plants. I felt so privileged to water her delicate asparagus fern that stood on a 7-foot pedestal and trailed on the floor. We ate together, cooked together, walked together, talked together and slept together. If she grew weary of me, I never felt it. Her patience, soft voice, light touch and gentle manner were heavenly.

I used to love nighttime because I helped her prepare for bed. She wore her long hair in a roll at the nape of her neck. At bedtime, she would remove the u-shape hair pins with the wrinkles (you know the ones), let her hair down, and I would brush it. She would then twist it into one long braid, which hung down the back of her white shift nightdress. We slept like spoons, nestled against one another, under sheets smelling of sunshine, which we had washed and hung outside to dry.

Grandma Schmidt told me stories of her days as a farmer's wife and how she fixed sit-down mid-day dinners for farmhands during threshing season, big dinners for big men: roast beef, mashed potatoes and gravy, corn on the cob, vegetables from the garden, fruit from the orchard and homemade baked bread and pies. Grandma Schmidt referred to herself as a "meat and potatoes woman." Her cooking legacy to me is roast beef and gravy. Standing beside me in the kitchen in that big, white house, she guided me making gravy from the roast we had prepared: "Good gravy depends on a good roast. Remove the roast and add your potato water to the roaster. Mix flour with water, not cornstarch, when making the thickening. Remember to add the thickening liquid to the roast's juices before the mixture begins to boil, stirring every minute. Otherwise, you will have lumpy gravy."

As I describe her work on the farm, you might picture a robust, even heavy set woman. Grandma Schmidt was just the opposite. She was slight built and wiry. She had what she called a "lame" hip which affected her walking. I always noticed her arms; the upper part was slim but muscular and the lower part was sinewy (think of the Arm & Hammer soda box). She dressed plainly in a cotton, mid-length housedress for everyday and a silk, either black or navy, for dress. She wore no jewelry except her wedding band.

At least once a week, we would sit in the parlor of her big, white house on a maroon velvet sofa, side-by-side, as she carefully lifted from a cabinet a small brown reed basket, 7- inches in diameter. It was decorated on top with turquoise beads, coins and a cross. Inside were newspaper clippings: weddings, bridal showers, family reunions, church confirmations, deaths and births. I loved the one announcing my birth! The clippings prompted stories about birthday parties, dances at her farmhouse, deathbed vigils, children who died young from fevers and picnics at gravesites on Memorial Day where friends and family were remembered. Grandma Schmidt's jewels and riches were her newspaper clippings.

She came to live with us when I was in my teens. I have precious memories of those years also, but the years when I was very young are the most vivid and cherished. Grandma Schmidt died suddenly of a heart attack at age 86 while sitting in her rocking chair on the front porch of our house.

I inherited the round, brown reed basket with its riches. I hadn't looked at in years until now. As I sift through the clippings, the oldest, now yellowed and crinkled with age, is dated Jan. 24th, 1900. The title is "Wedding Bells" and it says: "The bride is the youngest daughter of Claus Miller, was born and raised in this neighborhood and is a lady in every sense of the word. She is the possessor of a pleasant disposition and a kind heart and is a lady of sterling worth and will prove a loving helpmate to her husband." Grandma Schmidt remained true to this description. Through her wealth of family relationships and stories and unconditional love, she taught me the joy of continuity in family and friendships and traditions, which have enriched my life.

Carlota Carpenter
Washington, DC

CHAPTER XV

Mar-Mar

Kezia Mary (Payne) Guffey

Date of Birth: January 29, 1901 – Date of Death: August 30, 1992

Maternal Grandmother

Mar-Mar

This is a story about my grandmother, Kizzie Guffey, or as we called her, "Mar-Mar." How she got that name can be blamed on me. You see, when one is very young, pronunciation skills are still being honed and some of the things you say just don't come out right, often to the delight of your parents. One example was when I cried, I would go "mooooooooooo," so naturally, my parents called me Moo. Probably around the same time, I couldn't pronounce the word "Grandma," so I referred to my maternal grandmother as "Mar-Mar." That's how she got the name, and my family called her that for the rest of her life.

Mar-Mar, like all grandmothers, wore her name with pride, and it suited her perfectly. She was a delightfully quirky and very original woman and was my favorite grandparent. My mother pointed out that she was an independent-minded woman and had her own way of thinking about things. As an example, she thought her given name didn't suit her, so she unofficially changed her name to Kizzie Marie Guffey. Who does that?! Turns out, I did.

Mar-Mar was born in Newport, Virginia, in 1901. It was always easy to determine her age; take the current year and subtract '1.' She lived in a lovely clapboard home in Oak Hill, West Virginia, and was fond of crossword puzzles, her Episcopal church (she was a strong alto), putting up marmalade and pickles, and reading Pogo and horror stories. She played basketball at Oak Hill High School, and there were only 13 members in her graduating class. Mar-Mar married a civil and mining engineer who worked the coal mines of West Virginia. Francis Guffey was a Marine during WWI and apparently suffered from mustard gas inhalation. He died of a stroke when I was two years of age so unfortunately, I never really knew him. Kizzie never remarried because she said she could never find someone as good as Guffey (she referred to her husband by his last name, not his first).

I was called Guffey as a child, but when I reached the first grade, the teacher told me my first name was actually Arthur, and that I had four names, and the first thing we were going to learn was how to write our names in cursive. So, here's me, four long names, zero writing experience, learning cursive, classmates giving me crap and oh, some jerks start calling me "Guppy." Learning from this experience, in middle and high school, I went by Art (easier to spell, less trauma), but some of my oldest friends call me Guffey to this day. My mother reminds me that her father was very pleased I shared that name with him. I wonder if she knew how much trouble it caused me.

Mar-Mar was a fun and interesting person, intellectually strong and politically astute. She was a good listener and well-read. We had many lively conversations about local and state politics, coal mining, and West Virginia history. She was a passionate Democrat (my father said she would vote for the Donkey if it ran) and wouldn't shy away from sharing her opinion about our elected leaders. She would complain mightily about the politicians running her state and the country; she used the word "crooks" a lot. She was a union sympathizer and an advocate for the coal miner. She'd talk about the dark days of mining, the killings at Matewan and the crooked companies running people's lives. These conversations intrigued me and gave me a sense of right and wrong and the complex times she lived in. As I grew older, I found myself looking at things with a cautious eye, trying to determine motivation, who is right and why, the ethics of the situation, and so on.

She was skeptical and sometimes cynical, a trait my mom, sister and I share. She taught me about cooking, cross stitch, people and life. She led a simple life and never asked for much. While not poor, she lived frugally. When osteoporosis hunched her over, she still remained graceful and charming. She had a deep voice, and her laugh was more like a quick, adorable bark. I would take particular pleasure in getting her all worked up over nothing (that's what I do) as it was fun to hear her unique expressions and mannerisms.

She had a 1965 Chevrolet Corvair… the rear-engine car that handled like a boat (you know, the one that Ralph Nader had banned). It was fun to drive around town in with my sister. One of my first real tastes of freedom was driving that car through the streets of Oak Hill, without adult supervision, although my brother said it drove Mar-Mar crazy with worry to see me drive her 'temperamental' car.

The family would visit her a few times a year. The car ride was always an adventure because driving up and down twisty mountain roads usually made my brother carsick (he never overcame his glass stomach reputation). Also, we didn't eat at restaurants along the way; we ate at roadside tables: mushy bologna sandwiches and warm lemonade. McDonald's Hamburgers was the new, cool thing then; but noooo, Dad was too cheap.

When we got to Oak Hill, my brother, sister and I would play on the train tracks at the bottom of the hill. We'd come home with some treasures we'd find (like coal), and we were filthy from coal dust and grease, but Mar-Mar didn't care. One time the engineer of the local freight train saw us playing, and he stopped to take us for a ride. You should have seen the look on my dad's face when we waved to him from the locomotive as he drove by; priceless!

Mar-Mar took pleasure in the little things… flowers, words and the way an artist did something she found cute. My mom is a lot like her in these ways …me, too. She had a lovely yard and nice gardens with rabbits, birds, and other critters. Mar-Mar had apple trees, and we loved to eat crabapples and regrettably, the occasional worm. She had peeling birch trees by her dining room window. We learned that Indians made canoes and paper other cool things with birch bark, so we often peeled off a few strips and drew pictures and stories on the bark. My mom loved it when we got creative. The next time we'd visit, one of the first things we'd do is see if it was time to peel off a few more strips of bark.

A voracious reader, Mar-Mar would write in the margins of books, commenting on what she read. Her crossword puzzle word book was quite a sight: dog-eared with a broken spine and little notes all over the place. This was a valuable book, and my mother still has it. Sometimes we'd work the crosswords with her because the Fayette County Tribune didn't have the most challenging crossword puzzles. Mar-Mar was thrilled when we would bring her puzzles from the *Washington Post* or *New York Times*.

She only had one bathroom, so we all had to share. The floorboards of Mar-Mar's home were old pine, and the finish wore out in spots. We were warned to wear shoes or socks in the house because if you didn't, you usually got a splinter. Items from relatives (pictures, a parlor grand piano, silver, fine china and glassware, books, etc.) were all over the house, and each piece had a story. I have some of these items today, and they serve as cherished reminders of my family and its history.

I can vividly recall Mar-Mar sitting on her couch, smoking cigarettes, doing her puzzles and reading. She would fall asleep for a while and then wake up with a snort and get back to her reading. She was a great cook and didn't use recipes. She wrote lots of letters. She taught us how to play bridge. She'd always send us $10 for our birthdays and Christmas… no more, no less. I still have her last check somewhere. She hated it when I wouldn't cash them and she'd call me to get it done so she could balance her checkbook.

My uncle's family moved in with her for a few years, and those were fun visits because my cousins were there. Uncle Bo was good to his mother. Mar-Mar never had air conditioning, so Uncle Bo invested in a few window units and that made summer visits much more pleasant. They had a pinball machine in the basement, and we spent hours playing (remember my Dad was too cheap to invest in this kind of family entertainment). They introduced Mar-Mar to a washer and dryer; before that, she went to the laundromat (or to her neighbor Lucille's) to do her laundry. The machines looked strange in her cobweb-filled basement since it was usually empty, except for a few shelves lined with jars of pickles and jellies she put up. When Uncle Bo moved out, the washer and dryer (and sadly, the pinball machine) went with them, but I don't think Mar-Mar cared a bit. Old people don't do a lot of laundry!

Probably my most cherished memories were when I used to go to visit when I needed a break from college. Oak Hill was an hour away from Virginia Tech, so it was an easy trip. We would spend time playing cards, socializing and drinking Brandy Alexanders. Occasionally she'd take me out for a nice dinner at the Golden Corral (Oak Hill is not a big place!). Sometimes I would bring my girlfriend with me for a weekend visit since we both needed a good meal and a quiet place to study.

One time we got to talking about girls, relationships and ah, sex (I blame the Brandy Alexanders). Anyway, the conversation went into a little too much detail, and she let out this bark, made a funny face and said something like "What the hell, you did what?" I thought to myself, whoops, perhaps my dating habits are slightly different from hers. Anyway, she shrugged it off and muttered a few things and promptly got up and shuffled off to make us another pitcher of drinks. It's funny what memories stay with you.

Toward the end of her life, she suffered a stroke, and we moved her in with my mother at her home in Potomac, Maryland. By this time, she was in her 90s, and age had taken its toll. Most of her friends had died, she was far from home, and she was giving up. She didn't get out of bed much, so we'd sit in her room and talk about anything and everything... she was still very sharp. I took my fiancé to see Mar-Mar, and they grew quite fond of each other. We hoped Mar-Mar would be strong enough to attend the wedding, but it wasn't meant to be. She died in that bed... a week after my birthday.

Kizzie was an original and delightful woman. I carry her skeptical eye with me; however, like her, I remain optimistic and take delight in the little things in life; like the stroke of a brush, the cuteness of a bug and the delight of seeing a rabbit in the garden -- even if it's likely eating your lettuce.

Arthur C.G. Hyland
Vienna, VA

CHAPTER XVI

Granny

Jeannette Louise Koster Detweiler Latham

Date of Birth: August 13, 1926 – Date of Death: January 30, 2014

Maternal Grandmother

Granny

My maternal grandmother, Granny, and I were very close both emotionally and physically. I was lucky because she lived nearby, within thirty minutes of my home in Fort Worth, Texas, where I grew up. When I was 10 or 12, she moved even closer to us, into a small apartment about five minutes down the road. My grandmother was German, Scottish and English. She was about 5'6" and shrunk to about 5'4" as she aged. She was neither skinny nor obese but slightly round in the middle and healthy looking. My most indelible memory of Granny was that she was emotionally available and always cooking up something delicious.

When I was very young, from about six to 12 years of age, I would spend weeks, sometimes all summer long, Christmas and Easter breaks with her. She really loved to cuddle and was so affectionate, unlike my mother who had a hard time expressing herself and still does. Granny and I would lie in bed and watch old movies – mostly Turner Classic Movies. One of our favorite holidays to share was New Year's Eve when we would eat popcorn in bed, watch those old movies until just before midnight and then change the channel to see the ball drop in Times Square, New York City.

My grandmother was so different from my mother in every way. Granny was outgoing where my mother was introverted. Granny loved cooking, art, going out, shopping, making things and being with friends. My mother was just the opposite – quiet, loved to stay home and read. Granny and I always had a great time together. She taught me everything about living: how to cook, how to clean, how to iron, she even taught me how to paint like an artist. I received my first painting lesson when I was twelve; we worked on two landscapes together. She loved working with oil paint, but she could also draw and worked with watercolors.

She loved to try new things and found ways to support herself being creative. She decorated cakes, made portraits of people and their pets, designed dresses, cooked delicious food for others...and so much more. Because my mother worked odd hours at the post office, Granny and I had a lot of time to spend together, and many of the freelance jobs she worked found their way into my psyche, making me the creative entrepreneur I am today.

I would say that becoming an artist myself definitely started with her influence and teaching me how to paint. She was self-taught and did not have any formal education in art even though she could have gone to college. She always encouraged me to pursue creative activities. She was so, so happy when I decided to attend art school. She was curious and liked to try new things on her own and wanted to hear about the tips and new techniques I was learning at school.

Granny was incredibly outspoken; if she did not like something, she would let you know. This is perhaps one of the reasons she married and divorced so many times. Despite the divorces, I really admired this tell-it-like-it-is quality in her. I grew up in the South where being direct was not something a lot of women did. Most women honed the fine art of passive-aggression. My grandmother was originally born in New York State, where folks are known for speaking their minds. As you can imagine, she ruffled quite a few feathers in her adopted state of Texas!

My grandparents divorced long before I was born. I do remember my maternal grandfather, John Henry Detweiler, very well. He was a gentle, kind man who loved fishing and golfing and remarried shortly after they divorced. Actually, my mother is a lot like him, gentle, quiet, non-questioning. He died suddenly of a heart attack when I was fifteen.

Granny was on husband number three, Bill Latham, by the time I was born in 1977. They divorced in the early 1980s, and she remained single for the majority of my life. There was a very short fourth marriage, but that was annulled after six weeks. With four marriages under her belt, she realized she was happier living alone and gave up on romantic love. Instead, she shared her love with me.

Granny was always very well put together. She grew up in an age where ladies dressed and put makeup on before they went out of the house. I felt she took that idea too far, to the point of being vain and sometimes detrimental to her health. That said, I understand why she insisted on looking good; it made her feel better. She always wore a short, red wig, like Lucille Ball, until it was not age-appropriate and we finally convinced her to find a new wig that matched her gorgeous natural silver color. Granny loved to accessorize with hats, scarves and gloves and wore them to church on Sundays or any time there was a party or gathering.

One crucial thing important to note is the life-changing event my grandmother experienced in 1972 or 1973, a few years before I was born. My grandmother suffered severe burns that covered about 70% of her body in a grease fire at home. The accident is important to the physical description of her as it scarred her both physically and emotionally. Granny was a beautiful woman, and this event was life changing, as it would be to anyone. She was beautiful to me, and I never noticed the scars at all. However, she was very aware of them and always wore long sleeves and scarves around her neck.

The version of the story I know is that it was a cold day in Texas during winter time. Granny wanted to create a little heat in the house, so she turned on a burner under a cast iron pan without realizing that it was filled with grease. She lay down to take a nap and woke up to a fire. She grabbed the cast iron pan with her bare hands as it was on fire and took it to the back door. She opened the screen door and tried to throw the pan outside, but the screen door swung back and knocked the pan of hot grease all over her. She ran outside wearing a nylon housecoat, which totally melted onto her body, and I guess she was on fire, too. She said she ran outside screaming and neighbors saw her and ran over with bedsheets and rolled her up in them to put the fire out. She survived and lived in an Intensive Care Unit for approximately six months. Granny had more than eighty skin grafts and other surgeries over the next decade.

During her time in intensive care, the doctors didn't expect her to live, and if she did, she was not supposed to walk again. They wanted to remove her hands and her feet because they were so badly burned but her husband at the time, Bill Latham, wouldn't allow it. He said, "NO, if you take off her hands and her feet that will kill her."

She was very proud of how she looked. The doctors allowed her to keep her extremities, but they too were forever changed. Granny was not one to take "no" for an answer, and she worked tirelessly to regain her mobility. Independence was the most important thing to her. She was able to function normally and pursue her interests after many years of recovery and physical therapy.

I lovingly called her my "bionic granny" because she also had a glass eye as a result of the accident. In addition to the eye, she had false teeth, fake fingernails, plastic joints and wore support hose. At night, she would go through her bedtime routine and "take herself apart" before bed. We would joke that she lost her super powers at night and would regain them in the morning when she put herself back together.

What my grandmother left me is a love of life, to be creative and to really appreciate every single day we have. I have never met anyone like her – someone who had such a strong will to live – she loved every day of her life. Granny really fought for her life, and she was aware of just how precious that was to her. I also think the legacy that she gave me was to be tolerant of others and to really love everybody. I had strange-looking friends when I was a teenager, and she loved them all. She never said you cannot hang out with that person – she wanted to invite that friend over for coffee.

The most important thing about her and our relationship on an emotional level is I never felt like she was judging me. I could tell her anything, and she would respond to me as a friend. She never scolded me or told me I was bad. I don't remember ever being punished or disciplined. If I had a problem or question, and I needed someone to talk to, she was the person whom I called.

In my family, I am the only one that experienced this relationship with her. The others have very different positions and opinions of her but mine was truly only positive and full of love. Granny had three children, two daughters, one being my mother and a son. Her relationship to her children was very complicated and difficult; during the last fifteen years of her life, my aunt and uncle stopped speaking to her. There was a falling out and she did not see those two children or her grandchildren for the remainder of her life – almost 20 years. It was heartbreaking for me to watch her grieve over those relationships.

I am truly blessed because of the great relationship I had with my grandmother, and my cousins missed out on that. When she was alive, I did not appreciate how much she loved me. She would write me love letters, which I took for granted. But now, I have lots of things around the house to remind me of her such as her ashes in a Cafe Vienna coffee can (her favorite drink!), jewelry and paintings by her. These artifacts make me smile and help me remember to be grateful for the experiences we had, the love she shared with me, and the openness she fostered in me.

Amy Williams
Brooklyn, NY

CHAPTER XVII

Mama Pearl

Pearl Magda Hughey White

Date of Birth: September 6, 1903 – Date of Death: August 29, 1993

Maternal Grandmother

Mama Pearl

Thoughts of My Grandmother

When I think of Mama Pearl, my mother's mother, I know she loved to write and was very intelligent. Remarkably, she was a feminist, although we did not have that particular word in our vocabulary yet. For example, she would read an article or biblical scripture and write out her thoughts. One way her feminism expressed itself was that she marked out 'him' or 'man' and wrote in 'person.' Mama Pearl was very hardworking and a 'stay at home mom' until all of her three children were in school. She worked in the JP Stevens Cloth Mill in Piedmont, South Carolina, and was the overseer of the cloth room. At this time in history, it was very unusual for a woman to be the overseer of men. One of the things that she always said that I will never forget was, "Ignorance is worse than bad manners." Bad manners were the second sin while ignorance held first place. She considered it quite intolerable. Her contention was that if one were poor, this was no excuse as one could go to the library. If one could not read, one could seek a teacher to teach them. She had a strong belief in self-improvement and that society did not owe anyone anything. She was extremely independent and held other people to her same high standards.

Mama Pearl had a very strong work ethic. When I got married, one of the little "pearls" of wisdom she gave me (and I did not understand it at that point in time) was that I should always have a job because staying home and keeping house was one of the most horrendously boring things in the world that women had to do at that time. The worst thing about keeping house was the tedium of having to do the same things all over again the next day, the next week, the next month, the same thing over and over again. But while she hated it, she did housekeeping better than anyone I've ever known. Whatever she did, she did it to the extreme best of her ability. That principle has always stuck with me throughout my life, and although I have tried to instill it in my own children, I feel I have not done as good of a job as she would have done.

She loved entertaining and she really enjoyed the *process* of getting everything ready. It was my job to polish the silver from the age of about eight and up. To this day, I have great memories of talking at the dining room table while polishing everything in sight. She loved getting out the nice china – not for every occasion, but for someone's birthday or special holidays.

My grandfather retired and later died in his late 50s. Afterwards, Mama Pearl bought one of the early VW bugs (Beetles) and learned how to drive. We loved that the official color of her car was Pearl White – just like her namesake. She worked the rest of her life mostly in the mill but later in a downtown department store and drove herself to work in that Beetle. Years later she married an Englishman, a Methodist minister named Percival Elliott. I was thrilled to have a family member who was from England, had family there and here in the U.S. They went back several times to visit his family there, and some of them came here also. This was when the Beatles and Rolling Stones were huge, so I vicariously was associated with true English customs and foods.

I have never been overweight, and I believe the reason was and still is because of her attitude toward being overweight. I distinctly remember one Saturday morning passing by the bathroom and seeing Mama Pearl on the scale weighing herself, saying "Well, that's enough of that!" For three days, she only drank juice because she was three pounds over her ideal number on the scale. Impressed me, that willpower!

I spent the night with her – every other weekend from as long as I can remember in childhood. Actually, I would spend the weekends with every other grandmother every other weekend. Let me explain that I had five grandparents – one grandfather and four grandmothers (two grandmothers and two great-grandmothers) all in the same small town. I did not realize until I was in my 40s that this is how parents got a break from their children! I consider those weekends spent with grandparents a huge factor in forming the person I have ultimately become as an adult. All children should be so blessed. She wasn't really a "touchy-feely" kind of grandmother but was affectionate with hugs whenever I came over to her house, even if I had seen her last that very morning.

Mama Pearl was a really good cook. When I got married one of my favorite presents was a "whapping spoon" from her. It is a plain wooden spoon worn silky-smooth to be used as an utmost last-ditch method of bringing your husband around to your correct way of thinking. I have actually had to say a few times, "Don't make me get out my whapping spoon!" and it amazingly works on children too!   It will be passed on to my daughter when she marries. I still have her cast iron skillet that my great grandmother had and her spatula, which was razor sharp. The metal had worn so thin, and the red paint had come off, so my husband had it welded back like new. I also have several of her casserole dishes, which I love using as they bring back memories of many happy family dinners together. Before I got married, I did not have a whole lot of kitchen things on purpose because I always wanted family things instead of new ones. It means so much to me to be able to hold the glasses we all drank out of and eat cereal out of the bowls I used as a child at her house. These objects are my treasures.

My grandmother had three children, and I was the first grandchild – the darling No 1. I was four years old when my sister was born, and I don't think I was ever jealous of her because I assumed everyone loved me the most. My grandmother was the oldest of six children and grew up with a lot of responsibility, which had a major influence on her personality. She believed people should be responsible for their actions yet also forgiving and kind toward others.

When Mama Pearl was in her 80s, she had to have one leg amputated below the knee as a result of poor circulation. This occurred the day after my first child, Andrew, was born. A few months later, she had the other leg amputated. When I was first married, my family lived in Florida and we would visit mainly during the summer. I would stay a week or two at my grandmother's home and then at my mom's home – making the rounds. One night Mama Pearl was in such pain, she was praying to die. She was begging for God to take her. This was the first time I had ever seen her as a vulnerable person, as she could not stand the pain. But she came through, strong and determined as ever, and refused to have someone stay at night. She was in a wheelchair then, and she would have assistance until about 4 pm. This all occurred when she was in her late 80s!

My grandmother always said that true manners were a sign of class. My grandfather was a magistrate, which meant they were important people in town and her grandchildren had better know how to act in public. I vividly recall having to walk around with a book on my head for good posture. She lived in a regular white wooden house, and the staircase was long with lots of stairs. I practiced walking up and down the stairs without looking down. Much later when I was in college, I recalled seeing Audrey Hepburn in the movie *Roman Holiday* going down a gorgeous staircase into a ballroom. She never looked down. I wondered if she had a grandmother like mine. Mama Pearl would say, "When you enter a room, you have to enter with confidence and always stand straight. If you look like you are confident, you will be, and others will think you are." Also, how a person conducts themselves in public is a representation of your family.

I do believe that all southern grandmothers are strong. The steel magnolia is indeed true. They are stronger than steel under that soft exterior. But kindness would always come through with Mama Pearl, and she believed it was a social responsibility to be kind to others. I was taught that if there is something you can do to make life better for others then you are obligated to follow through and take action. I think that may be the core of why I am a Head Start teacher. I believe she would tell me today that I have done well in life, made good choices, and that she has always been proud of me, my posture *and* my manners.

Rebecca Pearson Feldman
Summerville, SC

CHAPTER XVIII

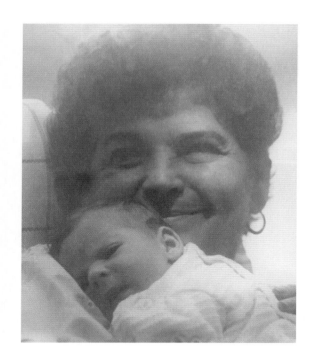

Grams and Beth

Nonna and Beth

Molly Horowitz

Date of Birth: November 28, 1922 – Date of Death: April 28, 2004

Paternal Grandmother

Grams

Grandmothers are truly special people. I am fortunate enough to have had an amazing bond with my paternal grandmother, whom I called 'Grams', until she passed away when I was in high school. I am equally as grateful for the relationship that I have with my maternal grandmother, whom I call 'Nonna.' I hope to share with you a little bit about these two amazing women as I reflect on why they are so important to me.

I had a very special bond with my paternal grandmother, who I called 'Grams.' I was in high school when my Grams died, and it was difficult as we were incredibly close. She always called me her "angel." It was our tradition to speak every weekend and catch up on all the things that were going on in our lives. She was my biggest fan, strongest supporter, and was there for me though thick and thin. My Grams was such a loving person but was also very strong-willed and determined. Toward the end of her life when she was in so much pain, sometimes she would cry. When I asked her what was wrong, she said it was because she was so happy to be with "her angel." I knew even as a young child how much pain she was in, but she never wanted me to know and always kept a smile on her face. It reminds me, to this day, how important it is to be grateful for relationships you have and not to focus on pain or negativity.

When Grams died, there was a rainbow at her funeral that touched me for some reason. It felt different from other ordinary rainbows that I had seen. Now, every time I see a rainbow, I know that my Grams is watching me and smiling, and that *she* has become *my* angel. Recently I was on a one-way plane ride to Colorado, where I was following my dreams of living in the Western United States, and when I looked out the window, there was a rainbow. I got chills instantly, and I knew in that very moment that Grams was smiling with pride. Even though she is no longer living, I will always feel eternally connected with her and her beautiful spirit. Her unconditional love, strong will to survive any illness, and her zest for life will continue to inspire me for the rest of my life. I can still hear her voice telling me I will always be her angel. I can smell the scent of her perfume. I can feel her soft touch as she would rub my back to help me fall asleep. Those experiences are more important than any gift you could ever receive, that no one can take away.

Mary Elisa Maruca

Date of Birth: September 28, 1933. Not deceased.

Maternal Grandmother

Nonna

I feel very fortunate to have a loving relationship with my maternal grandmother, "Nonna." Nonna is 'grandmother' in Italian, and she is still very much alive, as is our strong bond. Nonna raised five girls and helped to raise seven grandchildren. I would best describe her as nurturing, wise, witty and very practical. She never received a formal education, yet she has the keenest sense of what people are like – more than anyone I know. She even has premonitions and can assess any situation and 'call it' for what it is. One unique bond that my Nonna and I share is food and most importantly, how to show love through food. Whenever I was sick, she knew that her delicious homemade chicken soup would cure me.

Anytime I had a boyfriend or friend coming over for a visit, she would ask, "What is his or her favorite meal or dessert?" Sure enough, she would have whatever it was ready on the table. Food is her passion, and she has passed down this way of showing love to me through the years. Nonna and I bonded over food when I was a little girl and have shared this passion ever since. She has shared recipes with me that I will cherish forever. Watching her cook is amazing as nothing is ever written down; its all "old school" and by instinct alone. Every time I eat her homemade tomato sauce and peach jam, it's like I am eating it for the first time, and my senses explode with happiness and nostalgia. Some of my favorite recipes that Nonna made were her mouthwatering homemade tomato sauce, chicken parmesan, manicotti and lasagna rolls. Everything is made with one special ingredient: love. My mom created a memory DVD with photos of the tomato sauce making process, so that our family will always cherish this tradition. Everyone in the family gets several jars of this delicious sauce. Nonna used to have three refrigerators – one for cooking, one in the basement for baking and an extra freezer in the garage for 'extras.' Some cooks are good at cooking, and others are good at baking, but my grandmother excelled at both.

Nonna has become very modern and technologically savvy. The family gave her an iPhone for Christmas, and she and I have been texting, sending picture messages, and FaceTiming ever since! Everything that has to do with technology simply amazes her, and she is eager to learn. I recall one day when I called her from my cell phone, and she shockingly said, "I was just going to FaceTime you!" I told her, "All you have to do is think about that person, and the phone rings." She really believed me for a minute, but then I just had to tell her that I was only kidding! We laugh about that to this day and also enjoy reminiscing about times when I was little, and I would ask her which was her "good" ear. She had whooping cough as a young child, so she was deaf in one ear. We would sleep in the same bed when I would stay over at her house. I loved it and still remember it so vividly. She was about an hour from where my mom, dad and I lived, which was not that far at all. But I never wanted to leave her when I had to return to my home. Our time together, when we looked at pictures, cooked together – simple things – I just never wanted to leave her.

I hope that I will be lucky enough to be blessed with grandchildren of my own one day so that more memories and traditions can be kept alive. I think the greatest gift that you can give someone is honoring him or her in a special and meaningful way. This essay is just one very small way of saying "thank you" to both of my grandmothers by recognizing how truly lucky I am to have had strong relationships with such beautiful women.

Beth Horowitz
Denver, Colorado

CHAPTER XIX

Grandmother and her two grandchildren

Clara V. Chaudoin Porter

Date of Birth: March 09, 1888 – Date of Death: November, 1990

Maternal Grandmother

Grandmother

My first memory of my grandmother was when I was in her house and when I was a young child in her home, in Washington, D.C. I went to 2nd grade in the school right across the street. My mother and stepfather were living with her for a year until we found our own place. I called my mother's mother, 'Grandmother.' She was born on March 9th, 1888, in Ozark, Missouri, and died in November of 1990, on Thanksgiving Day of that year. She lived to be 102 and nine months old.

Her parents had eleven children, and she had eight grandchildren from her four children. She was American born of pure French blood. I don't think she spoke French because we never asked and she never spoke it in front of us. Ironically, her mother's name was 'America.' She was loving, caring, doting, happy, hard-working and awesome. She was special to me because she was a real human being and I noticed it at a young age. She had left school with a 3rd – grade education to stay at home with her mom to help raise her siblings. Later on, she divorced my grandfather, left Missouri, and came to start a new life in Washington, DC.

Grandmother got a job working at Safeway, as a cashier. When they found out how old she really was, they forced her into retirement at age 65. In a little time, she got a job as a receptionist for a physician. She maintained a long, semi-friendship with the physician's wife after he died. When Grandmother was in a nursing home, this same friend visited her in a chauffeured Rolls Royce.

I recall Grandmother telling me that she had purchased two beautiful, single beds with intricate wood designs on the headboards from another friend. The beds also had footboards as well. The best part of this story is that these very same beds were in the movie, "Gone with the Wind" and they are now in my home.

I remember that Grandmother took me to California on the train to visit her sister when my mother was getting remarried. But I was quite young, and I think we stayed for only a week. I also went with her on the train to take my two nieces home to Florida after a visit when I was in my thirties. We all had a great time on the train.

I have many memories of her cooking and the two of us having lots of laughter together. Everything she made was from scratch! She was an awesome cook and made her own biscuits, cakes, pies, her own gravy for mashed potatoes and made the best fried chicken ever. One thing she always did for me when I was quite young was to keep a dozen cans of my favorite foods in her home. Butter beans were one of those favorite foods of mine. They were stored in her basement, and to this day, I can see the two of us going down there with that ledge on the right-hand side and an L-shaped stairway. I always ate everything on my plate and she called me the 'garbage disposal' of the family. If you did not make a "shiny plate", you got no dessert.

Grandmother's composure was amazing. I do not remember when she lost her temper. She was very even-tempered and quiet. When one of my uncles died of a massive heart attack in his early sixties, my mom, brother and I went to her apartment to tell her. She just sat down with the greatest calm and stared into space and did not say a word. She had a look of deep sadness, probably shed a tear or two and then, as a proper woman from the Midwest would do, she got up and offered to fix a snack and something to drink and went on with her life. I remember thinking I was glad my younger brother saw this, hoping that this would teach him another lesson in growing.

She was very tall and stately, but eventually old age took its toll. Even though she did not have the education and with her Midwestern living, she knew how to dress immaculately. She knew how to put things together which included her earrings, her necklaces, and her clothing. She loved playing Chinese Checkers, loved the newspaper and the comics, and in her 90's, she would bob her head to the rock and roll music in my car. We stopped one time at Roy Rogers and had fried chicken. Again, she would bob her head in rhythm to my rock and roll music. Would you believe Mick Jagger and the Rolling Stones! She loved people and laughter and never drank or smoked at all. She maintained a beautiful figure all her life and was healthy as a damn horse until dementia set in at age 'ninety-nine plus' years old. Grandmother could climb the stairs up until the end with no assistance. I live in a three-story townhouse where she lived from 1984 until she was nearly 100 years of age. One time my mom, my friend Joe and I were with her, and she looked at me, smiling, and said, "Who are you?" This happened in her bedroom in my home, which crushed me. It wasn't long after that time, that we placed her in a nursing home.

Grandmother was a very strong woman, emotionally, and I never remember her depressed – that I knew of. Her spirit was always that of joy and laughter with all her family. She was my inspiration and our family's rock.

Phil Beasley
Alexandria, VA

CHAPTER XX

Meme

Marie Lavigne

Date of Birth: Unknown – Date of Death: Died in early 1960s.

Maternal Grandmother

Meme

I am of French ancestry, and my maternal grandmother, Marie Lavigne, was born in Lyon, France. She died in her early 70s and her one and only child, my mother, pre-deceased her. I was 20 years old when my mother died.

I did not see my wonderful grandmother many times. However, I remember when I was 15 years of age, I went to spend a month with her during my summer vacation. She and my grandfather were retired at this time and lived about an hour from Lyon in the countryside. In their retirement, they moved to a larger house with a beautiful garden in the back where the air was clear and you could see the mountains of Switzerland. Her garden displayed all colors of roses, carnations, and other flowers; many vegetables, a prune tree and a cherry tree. I remember climbing on the cherry tree and picking all those cherries.

We had fun, talked and talked, and on Saturdays, we took the bus to the next town, to a fresh market. We bought things, had lunch, ate chocolate on the way back home -- one more piece, one more piece, so that there was nothing left at the end of the bus ride. In the evenings, we listened to the radio and played card games at night-time. There was no television at that time and we stayed outside enjoying the garden. I vividly remember we were like mother and daughter, which for me was a special treat. She loved to cook, sew, embroider, crochet, knit and was a very handy woman. I learned at lot from her.

My grandmother was shorter than I, and I especially remember her beautiful blue eyes. She had white curly hair and took good care of herself. She was elegant when she and my grandfather went out for the evening.

I was 21 years old when I married, and my husband and I visited with my grandmother. He loved her, and they were funny together. While I did not see her often, we wrote to each other. I sent her photos of my son and that made her a proud great grandmother. Sadly, however, she died not long after my son was born. He was still a baby. I have two children and now, four grandchildren.

When I think of my grandmother to this day, I still feel her love and her affection. Once, she bought me a beautiful ring - she was very giving. I shall always remember her with love.

Madeline B.
Maryland, USA

CHAPTER XXI

Granny

Ruby Camilla Tabor McCarty

Date of Birth: April 13, 1895 – Date of Death: January 24, 1974

Paternal Grandmother

Granny

My first memory of my grandmother relates to the first home I lived in. I remembered it was a duplex. My mom, dad and I lived on one side of the house, and my grandmother and grandfather lived on the other side. My father was her only child. I was the first grandchild, and I remember being in a walker. I could go out the back door, and then I could go right into Granny's back door. My grandmother was always a presence as long as I can remember from being a little child. She was a real 'no frills' kind of person. She did not dress up, did not wear makeup, and always had a really simple hairdo. My grandmother could put the roof up on her own house! She was an avid gardener, planted her own vegetables and when we had chicken soup, she would catch the chickens and cut off their heads. This all took place in Los Angeles where she settled in the early 1900s with her family.

My grandmother was born in Morgan City, New Orleans, Louisana, and she grew up in the swamps. Her mother was a mid-wife and used to travel by those flat bottom boats through the swamp, and she would deliver babies for people in the neighborhood. I found out when I was 50 years old that my grandmother and grandfather were African American. I never knew this growing up as it was hidden from us and we were pretty naïve about race. Both of my parents were African American yet fair-skinned and passed as white. My grandparents on both sides moved from New Orleans where things had to have been pretty bad. In California, they passed as white.

When my father joined the service, and entered World War II, he passed for white. He wanted to be an Army Corps Engineer, and as a black man that was impossible as the army was segregated. It was not until years later when my father died that I discovered his birth certificate said he was a Negro. When I talked to my grandmother's relatives, I learned of the pact they made, which was that they would pass for white. You have to understand that in those days discrimination was commonplace, and to ensure a better future for their family, they did what they felt they had to do to get jobs and housing. As a child, my grandmother would take me and my two younger sisters traveling on the bus to Venice, California. She would take us with her to visit her brothers and sisters, but they never came to visit us, in our part of the city. We only went there. We were raised pretty much color blind. Color blindness to me was that we never saw someone's skin as being an identifier. We had family who were black, and we had relatives with red hair. It was just the way it was. I attribute that to my grandmother who, even though she had suffered prejudice, never shared that with us.

My grandmother gardened, so we used to garden with her. But my grandmother was also a lot of fun when it came to her granddaughters as we could do anything. She would say, "You want to smoke? Okay, let's go outside, and we will smoke." She showed us how to do it. She would let you try things. My grandmother was welcoming to every friend I had. She was very compassionate. When her sisters became ill and sick, we would get on the bus and go see them. My grandmother would take care of them. Nothing was sacred to her – she did not take too many things seriously. She always had a funny, irreverent story to share.

I remember going to her brother's home when he and his wife were on vacation. My grandmother was taking care of their house. She would let us play with all their grandchildren's toys and look for change under the sofa cushions. She would always tell us the story of the Mississippi River -- it would rise, and there would be a great flood. They would put mattresses on the dining room table – one mattress on top of another until it was near the ceiling and her father would get a boat and pass all the children out to safety and higher ground. My grandmother never drove a car; she took the bus everywhere. She was notorious for always forgetting her teeth, and we would have to go back to get them for her.

My grandmother was very slight – maybe 5'4" and she never dyed her hair. She let it go gray and wore her hair in a page boy. I think she cut it herself. We always lived close to her, and as children and teenagers, we were always at Granny's house. When we starting dating, we always brought the boys to meet Granny. My grandfather was a fireman. He was one of the first black men hired by the fire department in Los Angeles. This was before any of us were born.

My grandmother was funny and had a very dry sense of humor. She helped raise a cousin of my father's, and he eventually moved away and got married. He would come back once a year at Christmas time to see my grandmother. He would bring Knottsberry Farm Jelly for her -- she had a good sense of humor about it. She would make fun of his wife by saying the wife was "putting on the dog" or trying to act fancy, which was something my grandmother would never do.

My grandmother taught us how to crochet and how to embroider (e.g., 'his' and 'her' towels) but never forced us to do anything. She was an awful cook. Everything was fun, and nothing was serious. She went hunting in Utah with her brothers once a year. They would go in the station wagon, and a deer would be on the top of the car when they returned home. This was a rare sight in Los Angeles. She also went crab fishing, would then cook, and we would cover the dining room table (which was a fancy dining room table with dishes) with newspaper and then enjoy the feast of crabs and artichokes. She would also make okra gumbo.

After my mother died, my sister and I went to New Orleans to see where our grandparents came from. One of the most memorable things for us was that we were in the taxi cab and the driver was talking in the same accent that my grandmother and her brothers spoke. We went into restaurants and recognized the same foods that Granny made. Everyone in New Orleans was making it too. When we went into the French Market, we saw mirlitons, a green bumpy pear-shaped squash. This squash was common in LA, but no one called it a mirliton, so we were very surprised that it was really called that and not something Granny had made up. She used many words that were from her New Orleans background, and we didn't know that.

We just thought she spoke funny and made food that no one else we knew had eaten. Family stories say that my great-great-grandmother was the mixed child of a plantation owner and a slave. This would explain why they were so fair – half white and half black.

My memories of my grandmother were that she was an affectionate person. She was always kind and never yelled or reprimanded us. Her home was just like her – comfortable and not fussy. She let us cook, she let us play dress up, she made doll clothes; she was everything a Granny should be. She moved in a quiet, confident way – working hard and not complaining. I know by her example that I learned to accept life in that same quiet way. I learned the value of hard work and not taking one's self too seriously.

I've always had a quote posted above my desk that reminds me of my granny every day. "Angels can fly because they take themselves so lightly…" G.K. Chesterton.

Karen Alonzo
Los Angeles, CA

CHAPTER XXII

Gaga

Left to right: Gaga, her two young sons and her grandmother

Florence Maud Goulden

Born: 1875 – Died: 1944

Paternal Grandmother

Gaga

Gaga was what I called her, my paternal grandmother, though her given name was Florence Maud Goulden.

She came from Preston, about fifty miles north of Liverpool, that great seaport in England's northwest. She married my grandfather Stanley Manson in about 1885, after a courtship which I have always imagined was "flowery," for her family were rose growers, and there was one song I always associated with her: "Come into the Garden, Maud."

Grandpa Manson was a pharmacist, and they started their married life in Waterloo, a suburb of Liverpool, in a roomy house above his chemist shop. That was where their two sons Donald and Norman were born and raised. I have vague memories of that old house. Grandpa was an old-fashioned chemist who eschewed all modern appurtenances like cosmetics. He would sometimes feed me with one or two sweet jujubes from a big jar behind his high counter.

Gaga kept chickens in a narrow back yard. My mother, Bunty, used to tease Gaga: "Oh, what a wicked woman you are! You give those chickens names, and yet you don't hesitate to cook them!" As you can imagine, these words made a strong impression on me, even if Bunty was only teasing.

Donald, my father, was a marine engineer who sailed the world throughout his life, and his mother, Gaga, was my favorite relative. My mother, Bunty, claimed that she spoiled me 'rotten.' This was in the thirties when I was born, in 1931.

Gaga had three sisters-in-law, the Aunties, who were Stanley Manson's spinster sisters who lived in a market town called Ormskirk. Their house was my second favorite place to visit. They were Elizabeth, Gertrude and Nettie. Lizzie and Gertie were schoolmistresses at the local high school, and Nettie kept house for them. Ormskirk was the

Lancashire market town where they'd all been born, and where their father had been head gardener of a local estate, Asmell Lodge. Perhaps that was the connection with the Preston rose growers that Gaga sprang from.

Gaga's means of 'spoiling' me meant that she fed me lots of sugar – in sandwiches, if you can imagine anything so odd. We would go into her kitchenette and make whatever I wanted. The sugars would lead to many visits to the dentist. Or she would shell the tiny fingernail-size shrimps from nearby Morcambe Bay, which I would gobble down as fast as they were shelled, so never would a pile form.

The downside was that she had instructions from my mother to give me a 'good big teaspoonful of Milk of Magnesia', because my mother seemed obsessed with my bowels. The Aunties too had the same orders, only their vile potion was Syrup of Figs. Both made me gag.

Gaga would read me from memorable books on the crowded book shelves at the house where she moved after Grandfather Manson died in 1938. We would sit side by side on the leather settee, in front of the fire, as she unfolded tales for my eager ears. There was one story about an isolated house far away from any town, that was visited by the four winds, and it was the invincible North Wind that caught my attention. The South, East and West winds seemed cowed, almost silent, before the howling of the dominant North Wind.

As World War II approached and my sister was born, the German bombs started to fall on Liverpool – particularly on the docks of the huge shipping port, about two or three miles away. I was sent to live with Gaga, who by this time had moved again, about twenty miles north to an elegant seaside town called Southport.

There, on Lord Street, Gaga surprised me with one amazing incident. I would have been about ten years old then, and as we walked along Lord Street – always bathed in sunlight in my memory and crowded with wonderful shops for its whole length. Then my upright and staid grandmother did something that surprised me. One moment I was holding her gloved hand, she in her straw hat with a rose decorating it, and her prim silk dress, proper handbag and lace-up-shoes. The next thing she was darting forward towards a man coming towards us. He was wearing a trilby hat, and he had a rolled-up newspaper under the arm of his checked suit.

"Are you Lobby Lud?" Gaga demanded.

"No, I am not!"

I was left with my mouth hanging open at my grandmother's strange behavior. I had never seen or imagined her accosting a stranger. She then explained to me what had happened. A national newspaper, *The News Chronicle,* had an advertising campaign wherein people all over the country were accosting men hoping to find this mystery man called 'Lobby Lud.' The prize for finding the right man was a whopping 1000 pounds, a huge sum in those days. This was the only time Gaga did anything so bold. It impressed me, for she was so mild mannered, ladylike and full of propriety.

Gaga was warm, yet a little reserved, as most people were in those days. I don't recall her spending any money on me, or giving me gifts, but she herself was a gift to a young girl - so fully did she give of herself to me. She did love to go to the movies, and there were about eight movie houses along Lord Street, on the other side from the shops. I can vividly remember seeing *Gone with the Wind* with Gaga, sitting next to her and holding her hand as the drama unfolded. The screen had a gleaming gold curtain in front of it made of gold loops with ruching. It was almost as impressive as the movie.

About this time the bombing had become dangerous, with nightly raids. Bunty took me to a shelter opposite our house, carrying my sister in her arms. But the atmosphere was too rowdy for her, and right in the middle of a raid she rushed out, with the air raid warden shouting at her. We dashed home through a night electric with sirens and search lights filling the sky. We ended up sleeping under my mother's grand piano.

It was then that mother decided that we had had enough. We were soon on a packed train to Scotland, pretty much beyond the range of the bombers. She took us to an island on the River Clyde called Cumbrae, where she had spent her childhood holidays, and still had an aunt. We remained on that wonderful island until V-in-Europe Day, when I marched behind the bagpipes through the little town.

It was then that Gaga had a stroke, and we rushed down to Southport immediately. But she was unconscious and soon died. Mother took me into her room, where Gaga was laid out, silent, lifeless and strange. This was my first experience of death. Neither did I feel much grief, for I do not think that at fourteen, I could understand death. However, I do remember that after the funeral, which I did not attend, there was canned salmon for tea. It seemed very special as everything always was about Gaga.

Joy Billington Doty
Journalist, *London Times, Washington Star*

CHAPTER XXIII

Abue and her grandson, Nico

Astrid Elena Guerrero Portillo

Date of Birth: September 15, 1962. Not deceased.

Maternal Grandmother

Abue

Because this participant is **nine years of age**, this chapter will be formatted a little differently than the others. The questions are in bold and asked of **Nico** by his mother. Listed below are his answers that are italicized.

Q: **What is your full name, Nico?**

A: *My name is Nicolas Martin Amaury Portillo.*

Q: **What is your grandmother's full name?**

A: *Astrid "Abue" Elena Guerrero Portillo.*

Q: **Is she your maternal or paternal grandmother?**

A: *She is my maternal grandmother.*

Q: **What do you call her?**

A: *Abue.*

Q: **Do you know what year she was born?**

A: *She was born on September 15, 1962.*

Q: **Do you have a photo of her and would you like others to see it?**

A: *Yes.*

Q: **Where was she born?**

A: *Abue was born in Colombia, South America.*

Q: **What is your grandmother like?**

A: *She is nice, she loves us, she likes to cuddle and play with us. She is funny.*

Q: **What is special about your relationship?**

A: *Abue treats me very special and gives me cool nicknames such as "Pancakes."*

Q: **Can you remember any special times with her?**

A: *When she jumps on me and eats me because I taste like blueberries. She likes taking me to the pool every day when we visited Colombia, and she likes the Colombian soccer team and she is very funny with me.*

Q: **Is Abue funny – is she serious – what is she like?**

A: *She is very funny, very elegant and smart and likes going to church a lot.*

Q: **Can you remember one thing you did together that you will keep in your heart forever?**

A: *I love her. She jokes around with me. Abue likes to take me on vacations and we enjoy the fast rollercoasters together.*

Nicolas "Nico" Portillo

Silver Spring, MD

CHAPTER XXIV

No Photo Found

Mary Geha

Date of Birth: circa 1890 – Date of Death: 1968

Maternal Grandmother

Mamma Mary

My grandmother, Mary Geha, was diminutive in stature, but a titan in spirit. Mamma Mary, as she was known to her grandchildren – all four of us – was born in Damascus, Syria, and emigrated to the United States as a child of nine or ten. The family – her mother, father, and two sisters – settled in rural Northwest Ohio. Her father, a cook in Damascus, eventually acquired a small candy kitchen on the public square in a little town, Paulding, Ohio.

Mary's formal education was sadly lacking; she never graduated from high school. She spoke English haltingly and read it very poorly. But she was smart. She always worked primarily in food preparation, and she found her niche as a pie maker. Mary met and subsequently married Joe Geha. They produced six children – all girls. One of the young Gehas, Lucille, died of a strep throat. Penicillin had not yet been discovered.

The Geha girls grew, attended secretarial school, and married. One of them, also named Mary, and my grandmother decided to purchase a restaurant – a small one that seated around 80 customers. They hired a day cook, and my Aunt Mary was the evening broiler cook. Of course, my grandmother baked the pies – all of them – apple, cherry mincemeat, lemon meringue, butterscotch cream, coconut cream, banana cream, and so on. They sold out every day – at a staggering price of 20 cents a slice. Mamma Mary would allow no one else to cut the pies – EXCEPT ME! I frequently had lunch with my schoolmates at Geha's Restaurant and was supremely flattered when she asked me to assist her.

I got my driver's license on my 16th birthday, and this event opened up many new opportunities for Mamma Mary and me. Although I was known by my friends for my heavy foot on the gas pedal, I was the paragon of safety when my passenger was Mamma Mary. Frequently I took her to Van Wert, a neighboring small town, to visit one of her doctors. She boasted of my driving skills to my parents. I don't think they quite bought that.

Among her many accomplishments was sewing. She was an excellent seamstress. For Easter one year she made a pink sheath dress for me. The only problem was that between the time she had measured me for the dress and its realization, I had added quite a few pounds. I managed to wear it, but it was close!

As Mamma Mary aged, her asthma, always severe, worsened. At that point, she joined her sister in Phoenix, Arizona. Subsequently, three of her five daughters, including my mother after my father's death, joined her there. I visited frequently until her death in 1968. I will never forget the times I spent with her. She was kind, loving, smart, capable and determined. When she died, God threw away the mold.

Suzanne Cavanagh, PhD
Washington, DC

CHAPTER XXV

Grandma and granddaughter, Susie

Elizabeth Mary Viscosi

Married name: Elizabeth Lauria

Date of Birth: November 6, 1924 – Date of Death: November 7, 2014

Maternal Grandmother

Grandma

My grandma was always my voice of reason. She had many quotes that she would recite to me -- "Que Sera, Sera, whatever will be, will be." "It is in God's hands." "He will take care of it." But one thing that she always told me that we lived by was "Don't give up the ship." She and I had matching shirts that had that quote on the back. She wrote that quote in every card and letter she sent me. She had an unbelievable sense of humor and ended every phone conversation with, "Susie, always remember… Don't give up the ship. And I said SHIP!" "Love, Love."

I was born in upstate New York where my grandparents (both maternal and paternal) lived their entire life. I lived there until I was four years old and then my mom, dad, brother and I moved to New Jersey. So, from such a young age, my relationship with my grandparents was always long distance. I grew up in New Jersey, but every holiday, every summer, and other times in between, we got to see each other. My grandparents would also make special trips down to New Jersey to come and watch my brother and me when our parents were out of town. Our long-distance relationship was the only thing I knew. This did not get in the way of the strong connection my maternal Grandma Lauria and I had. As I continued on my own life journey and graduated high school, I decided to go to college at Millersville University in Pennsylvania. During my time in college, I made sure I would talk to my grandma over the phone at least three times a week. I took a semester abroad when I was in college in Liverpool, England. It was difficult to communicate with anyone in my family for those four months. From the time difference to the process it took to call, it was all very challenging. The only person I really talked with was my mom, and she would fill the rest of the family in. At that time when I was studying abroad, my paternal grandma, Grandma Bouchard, had passed away. The distance was very difficult for me as I was not there when she passed and did not have the comfort of my family nearby. Once again, long distance was all I ever knew.

My Grandma Lauria was about 5'2" but as she and I both got older, I definitely became taller than her, as I think she lost a few inches along the way. She was very domestic, cleaned the house daily and would mop her kitchen floor every morning. She was always keeping things tidy and clean. She had a sheet cover over her couch cushions. The second people got up from the couch, she would fix it so that there were no wrinkles and it looked presentable. She was a very good cook – not a baker, but a cook. She cooked a fantastic number of Italian dishes. Those Italian dishes still live on in our family. Her dessert that she would make was always rice pudding, and that was her signature dish. Cooking wasn't the only thing my grandma enjoyed. She also loved watching baseball (the Yankees), golf, *The Young and The Restless, The Ellen DeGeneres Show, Wheel of Fortune, Jeopardy,* and much more. However, television is not what interested my grandma the most. She enjoyed reading and would get lost in reading book after book. I admired that about her so much.

This maternal, witty, Italian grandma of mine was the most kindhearted woman and extremely generous. She was the kind of person that others were envious of. She was the most nurturing and compassionate person I knew. She worked so hard to make everyone around her happy. She filled her home with love and an enormous amount of patience. She and my grandpa had five children, my mother being the oldest. Out of the five, there was a set of twins who were born on my mother's birthday years later. My grandparents were the typical middle-class family and always worked extremely hard to provide for their family and community. I remember this story that my grandma told me. She would ask my grandpa if she could buy something for her family and he would say, "If you think we can afford it, go ahead." They never let money get in the way of their relationship or any aspect of their life. They put their children first and showed them that love, loyalty and believing in God were more important than anything money could buy. Our family was blessed to have such dedicated grandparents (the glue), to guide us in the right direction and teach us all of the life lessons that they had to share. Their marriage of 61 years is a true reflection of their commitment they had with one another.

After I graduated from college, I returned to New Jersey for two years and started my career as a Special Education Teacher. After those two years, I had decided to make a big move to the other side of the country, San Diego, California. I feel that my strongest connection with Grandma

Lauria came when I moved to San Diego. I talked to my grandma almost every morning on my drive to work. If I was not talking to her, I was talking to my mom about her. The funny part about it was that if I told my grandma a story about something going on in my life, like something at work, before I shared it with my mom, she felt so proud that she knew it before my mom knew it.

One of the best memories I have was when my grandma had the opportunity to come to San Diego with her two daughters – my mom and my aunt. It was a girl's trip and only my grandma's second time on an airplane. This trip was in April 2011, which was about nine months after my grandpa passed away. I never thought I would have the opportunity to have my grandma see where I lived. She very impressed, but she was a part of that older generation where one's family lived near one another. It was difficult for her to see that I lived so far away, and I understood why she felt that way. After all, my aunts, uncles and cousins lived within miles of my grandma. It was so nice that she got to come and she could finally visualize what I had been explaining to her over the phone every day. After they left, I put together a photo book for my grandma so that she could show all of her friends back home. The photo book captured the amazing time we had and the memories that were made. It was a trip that will never be forgotten and will be cherished forever.

My grandfather died four years before her. It was ironic in that she was deceased on 11/7 and he died on 7/11. From the second he passed, my grandma had a very difficult time--- from then on and going forward. Those four years were not easy for my grandma. I think that was probably the first time I ever saw my grandma cry. It was nice that she felt comfortable enough to let her emotions show in front of me.

When I think of my grandma, the first thought that comes to my mind was her strong faith in God. She had a special relationship with God and practiced her faith each and every day. The last few years of my grandma's life, she would always say, "When it is my time I want to be blown out like a candle." And that she was. My Grandma Lauria passed away on the day after her 90th birthday. She was comfortable, at peace and simply satisfied with the great life she lived. She always said, "God has your path already paved for you…you need to trust and believe that He will guide you in the right direction."

Today I am left with such amazing memories of all of my grandparents, and feel so fortunate for their influence in my life. I now have both of my grandmas' engagement rings that I wear together every single day, and it is a true reminder of their lives that I hold so close and dear to my heart. It is ironic how these rings fit so perfectly together and almost look like they were made to be worn together. I believe it was 'meant to be.'

Susie Bouchard
La Jolla, California

CHAPTER XXVI

6.27.37

Auntie holding her granddaughter, Alexandra Scheele Ryan (Sandy)

Maria Kathryn Martin McCormick

Date of Birth: July, 1884 – Date of Death: October, 1955

Maternal Grandmother

Auntie

I called my grandmother 'Auntie,' her choice. She did not want to be called 'Grandmother' or 'Grandma.' In my case, my grandchildren call me 'Sandmom.'

The first memories of my 'Auntie' were the summer after first grade in 1942. My mother, sister and I moved to Detroit, Michigan, to live with my grandparents, an idyllic arrangement for two little girls. My father was overseas in the European theater during World War II. I was five years old, and my sister was two years old. My mother and her mother, Auntie, were very close. My paternal grandmother died before I was born.

My parents met at the University of Michigan. My mother was a dental student, and my father was an undergraduate. They married in 1929. My father went to medical school in Detroit, and my mother established her dental practice. For those next five years, they lived with Auntie and Grandpa. My uncle and his wife lived with them as well.

My grandparents were really fun people. Two little girls who had three adults— it was a great ratio to make plenty of fun and a happy family. My mother resumed her dental practice, working every day, so my grandmother took care of us. My grandmother had my sister, a two-year-old, all day. I was in second grade and remember all of this. My grandfather took me to school in his truck, and I would go back home after school. It was a very happy household. My mother would arrive between 5:30 and 6:00 pm. We all had supper together. My grandmother was a wonderful cook.

My grandfather was a cabinet maker. Trips to his shop were always fun. He made my baseball bat out of wood, and he taught me baseball. One night he brought home a puppy, a Scottish terrier, Angus. My sister and I were hiding on the stair landing, a habit we developed. Auntie was not thrilled about the puppy, but Maria and I were overjoyed. Our giggles were heard, and we were invited to meet Angus. Then it was back to bed. We also had chickens and two huge chicken coops in the backyard, many hens, and one rooster. They had a slanted ladder from the outside wire pens to climb into their garage roost. This was in the middle of

Detroit. It was such a happy place to be, and we collected eggs every day.

My grandmother sewed a lot of my sister's and my clothes. She would also make matching clothes for my dolls. She was raised by her grandmother when her mother died. Her grandmother had immigrated by boat from Southern Germany to Ontario, Canada, in 1850. Her father made a wooden trunk for her belongings. She made this voyage on her own at age 18. We still have the trunk.

Auntie was born in Canada, and at the age of 17, she immigrated to Detroit alone. She did what her grandmother did. She was working in the home of a family in Detroit when she met my grandfather. They were married, and she was age 20 when my mother was born. I do not know how much education she had, but she was very smart. She could have been a nuclear scientist had she had the opportunity. I can never remember my Auntie being angry but when she said 'no,' she meant it.

Auntie had a wonderful sense of humor and was good at cracking jokes. My mother, sister, my grandparents and I always had breakfast and dinner together. Auntie would wash the dishes, and my mother would dry them. My grandfather and uncle came home for lunch every day, and she prepared meals for the five of us, which we ate together at the kitchen table. Auntie and my mother were very close, and I ended up with a lot of their correspondence. There I learned that my mother and her brother called my grandmother "Zeus." I found this in her letters to my mother – she signed them with the letter 'Z.'

My grandmother was fun, energetic, had lots of friends, was a good sport and very adventuresome. She yodeled and could do the Cossack Dance in her sixties practically sitting on the floor. She was very organized, and she kept to a schedule of washing on Mondays, ironing on Tuesdays, cleaning on Wednesdays. On Thursdays, we went grocery shopping. She also belonged to a bridge group that met on Thursdays. She had lunch prepared for herself and her friends. My sister and I would go as well. I went in the summer, and my sister went all the time because she was so little. On Fridays, Auntie prepared for the weekend meals. I remember those Fridays because those were the days she would make sugar cookies, pies and cakes. It was fun to be a part of that. Auntie was little and cute. I never heard her raise a voice, and she and her daughter, my mother, never argued. They were in sync in terms of discipline and raising us in our household.

My grandparents were fun to be around because there was always activity or something going on. I can remember I used to sit on the back porch steps with my grandmother shelling peas. I can remember the time my grandfather came in the back door. My grandmother and I were in the kitchen. She was fixing dinner, and he handed her a bag from the butcher. This was a bag of oxtails, and she just exclaimed, *"Oh no, Alex."* He wanted her to make oxtail soup, and eventually, she did.

My grandfather and uncle built a cabin in Northern Michigan, in the woods. Throughout the spring, summer and fall, my sister and I would go up to the cabin with my grandparents. That was just great fun for us. We called it, "Up a North," my sister's invention. It was a lot of work for Auntie because there was neither electricity nor running water, a rustic life. A well was under the house, and my grandfather had rigged a pump. The cabin was one huge room. In the kitchen area was a pump but there were no bathrooms. There was an outhouse, a scary trip in the dark. The cabin had a living room-dining room: all was one big open space with no interior walls. The back part of the space had two curtains dividing it in half. The curtains made a "T" – one side was the girls' and the other was the boys'. My grandfather and my uncle built two huge queen-size bunk beds, each with an upper and a lower one. I don't know how my grandmother ever changed the sheets!

We would go to the ice house to get blocks of ice for the bottom of the ice box. I cannot remember what the stove was like, but it burned wood. Kerosene lamps and also flashlights were our light after dusk.

We were in Detroit for the war years and then we moved back to Washington, DC. My father was in Europe for four years. Auntie and my grandpa always came to visit us for Christmas and, in addition, several times a year. As soon as there were airplanes, she was the first one to fly. After that, they always flew to visit us.

In 1943, my uncle died. This was my Auntie's son and my mother's brother. He died very suddenly at 34 of a heart attack. His body was on view in my grandparents' home, a custom in those days. My grandparents were broken-hearted but showed such strength, a testament to their courage.

I am named after both my grandfathers and Auntie. Alexandra Martin Scheele. One grandfather was Alexander, and Auntie's maiden name was Martin. My paternal grandfather's first name was Martin. I took care of all the living grandparents. My sister is named Maria, Auntie's first name.

September 1955, I transferred to the University of Michigan in Ann Arbor, just 40 miles from Detroit. Several times I visited my grandparents. One weekend I drove them up to the cabin. That was a very special time. My grandmother died less than three weeks later in the middle of October. Devastating, so sad. She had a massive heart attack at age 71.

My goal in parenting and grandparenting has been to follow in the steps and mores of my grandparents and parents. I hope my grandchildren will have happy memories of me.

Alexandra Scheele Ryan (Sandy)
Washington, DC

CHAPTER XXVII

Nana

Eliza Springer

Date of Birth: 19th Century – Date of Death: Unknown

Maternal Grandmother

Nana

My grandmother, who was born in London, England, had a great sense of life and people. My mother and I were never close, but my maternal grandparents were wonderful. My maternal grandmother, whom I called 'Nana,' was Christian, and my grandfather was Jewish. They were Cockneys but did not have Cockney accents. They lived on the same block of flats where I lived in East London. The grandparents on my paternal side were not as close. They were born in Poland which was then part of Russia and both were Jewish. I am British and have also lived in the United States since 1957.

My grandmother was the love of my life. I adored her. She was a wonderful woman, gentle and with a great sense of humor. I loved both my grandparents, and I was an only child. My mother was not warm, and we did not have a close relationship throughout my life. I still remember those memories, and I am now 90 years old. But my grandmother was warm. She was not a show-off and just 'got on with life.' She was comforting, cuddly and affectionate, and that is what young children want and need. She did not burden me with anything to worry about. She simply treated me with great love and care.

Nana was not tall, not small, but of medium height. She had great white hair when she was very young and she wore it short. She wore fitted patterned dresses which I think were made of rayon. She had five children; my mom was the only girl, and the youngest. She was not a particularly good cook. My grandmother was not "sweet" but down to earth and always gave me good advice. My grandfather also gave good advice. He was a bookmaker. My memory is that I spent a great deal of time with Nana.

Nana was just a very steady woman. She sang, and while she did not have a great voice, we had fun singing songs of the turn of the 20th century, Cockney and music hall. One of those songs that I still recall was, "If you were the only girl in the world and I was the only boy…." There were so many great songs in the UK then. When we were going through World War II in London, it was actually a wonderful experience in that we were all together and we had the same sense of humor, which has never been seen again in that same way, since the war finally stopped.

My grandmother lived in East London – a true Londoner. My grandfather was lovely. I remember that he would always joke with me. If someone came to the door, he would tell that person that it was my birthday. He would say, "C'mon kid – it is your birthday." People would give me money, and later on, I realized it was his nature. He loved me dearly, and I loved him.

Other memories that I recall vividly were during the night. Most of the time I spent many nights with them. I even had my own bedroom. However, I would enter my grandparents' bedroom, and my grandfather would say, "Here she comes" and I would get in bed with Nana. She slept with me, and my grandfather would exit their bedroom and sleep in my bed.

About six years after I emigrated to the United States, in 1963, I was at a lovely party where I met my future husband. We were later married in 1965, in Portola Valley, California, by a school friend of my husband's in Budapest. When his friend grew up, he became a Priest and like my husband, immigrated to the United States. I still remember what I wore on my wedding day. I was dressed in a raw silk 'Jackie O Style' suit with a pillbox hat. It was made by a French dressmaker. At our reception, everyone went swimming, but I decided to keep my wedding suit on and enjoyed it immensely.

My husband and I settled in New York as he was teaching physics at Stony Brook University in Northern Long Island, New York. We bought a house near the University and my only child, a daughter, was born in 1967.

Recently, my first cousin got back in touch with my daughter and me. He now lives in Palo Alto, California. We connected after decades of time, and he would tell us stories about our past. He too lived in the same flats as well and his father was my uncle – my grandmother's son.

I have had a very full life and after all these years, I shall never forget the deep love my grandmother and grandfather gave me, which has brought me much comfort throughout my entire life.

Lesley Balazs
Washington, DC

CHAPTER XXVIII

My Iron Ladies!

Ama (means "paternal grandmother" in Cantonese)

Por Por (means "maternal grandmother" in Cantonese)

Pattama Phanphensophon

Date of Birth: August 21, 1921 – Date of Death: July 4, 2001

Paternal Grandmother

Ama (means 'paternal grandmother' in Cantonese)

My Iron Ladies

My father's mother, whom I call 'Ama,' was a tiny five feet tall and plump lady born on August 21, 1921. She was the eldest of the family, full of determination and independence. She traveled to Thailand from China during the Second World War with only 'a pillow and a blanket.' At the age of nineteen, she started her new life in a foreign country – alone.

I grew up with Ama, and all our fond memories revolved mostly around food. She was an incredible cook and taught me how to spot the freshest ingredients – "Do you know that fresh fish must have clear eyes and that green beans must not be wilted?" These were my very first memories about food. She constantly reminded me that "Good food must start with good ingredients and putting heart into cooking makes it exceptional." Over the years, I learned one important lesson – *always notice details and never cut corners in life. Everything you do, you must put passion into.*

She taught me the art of running a business. Her first business was a small restaurant, named Coca (means 'delicious'), serving home-cooked Cantonese food. Her hard work and passion successfully made the business grow into a 250-seat restaurant. Eating dinner together as a family was (and still is) our family tradition. It is the time when everyone can be together and share what we have done throughout the day. This culture has kept the family bond close.

It has been exactly ten years since my grandmother passed, but her voice and all the memorable conversations we shared over the dinner table still remain incredibly present. The smell and the exceptionally delicious taste of her cooking marked her natural talents. The passion for food and her warm hospitality came so naturally within her. She was simply loved by people around her. Although she is no longer with us, it makes my heart pulse with pride every time I talk about her; everyone always says, *"We miss her."* Her incredible legacy will be forever cherished.

Tsui Bik King

Date of Birth: September 4, 1927 – Date of Death: October 25, 2011

Maternal Grandmother

Por Por (means 'maternal grandmother' in Cantonese)

My maternal grandmother, 'Por Por,' was born in Vietnam. Very similarly, she was a very successful lady and very career oriented also. She was very, very graceful and the principal of a primary school in Hong Kong. Por Por was very organized and full of energy.

I think the fondest memory I have of Por Por is of her as a 75-year-old lady horseback riding. She was very elegant, quite tall and loved the beauty and color coordination of the equestrian life style. She was very sporty and was a basketball player when she was young. Por Por had two little dimples and a beautiful smile that would light up anyone's day. She worked until her late 40s and then retired. She used to live in Vancouver, Canada, and I visited her every summer until I was about 20 years old. She later moved to Thailand to live closer to us. Every weekend we would spend time together, shopping and eating.

She was a very outgoing person and very good at socializing. She loved to dance and sing, cigarette in one hand and wine glass in another. She often hosted dinner parties where all her close friends would gather and dance the night away. The energy in the room was incredible, and the sound of salsa music still sounds very clear in my mind.

She lived a very long and healthy life until her health began to deteriorate in her early 80s. One Sunday afternoon, when my mother and I took her out for an afternoon tea, she was having her favorite ice-cream, but it was very strange that she did not speak – only smiled. An hour passed, her body shut down, and she collapsed. We rushed her to the hospital, and she was resuscitated. She lived for three days and then passed away. We flew her body to San Diego to be buried, as it was always her wish to be reunited with her eight other siblings.

'Live your life to the fullest. Love the people around you. Smile and raise your glass to what you have in life' – Por Por left us with her last words.

Natalie Phanphensophon
Thailand

CHAPTER XXIX

Gramma

Four generations: Left to right: the mother of the author, the author,
her baby and her Grandmother, Gramma

Edna Barth Barrows

Date of Birth: May 1, 1892 – Date of Death: 1989

Maternal Grandmother

Gramma

Gramma was born in the Chicago area in 1892 of Swedish parents. She had no siblings of which I'm aware and was orphaned at a young age. She met and married my grandfather when they were both 20, and they lived in Hinsdale, a suburb of Chicago, until they retired to Florida in 1957. My mother was their only surviving child.

Gramma was a warm, loving woman – a Norman Rockwell homemaker, mother and grandmother. She managed the home, was a wonderful cook and baker, a prodigious gardener, a seamstress – and a collector of American primitive furniture and glass. She was an amazing woman, and I believe I knew that, even though in retrospect, I realize I didn't spend more than a few days with her periodically as a young child. In 1957, when I started high school, my grandparents retired to St. Augustine, Florida, and after that, we had only a few visits. One very special event was when Gramma, age 85, came to the Washington, DC, area to help celebrate my first son's birthday. That was really important to me – it was our last visit together – and I cherish the 'four generations' photo we took then.

There is no doubt – Gramma was my rock. My mother was a single mom and often traveled for her work. It was a treat for me to spend time with my grandparents in their home in Hinsdale. Gramma was always there, not just caring for me but sharing her wisdom and her skills.

I wish I were as good a cook and seamstress as she – that's my fault for not sticking with those life skills, which I no doubt viewed then as not important. And for years our little family spent two weeks every summer at a rented cottage in Northern Wisconsin. Gramma organized the all-day drive, complete with a picnic basket of snacks and lunch, and insisted that we stop for ice cream at one spot along the way. Another stop was at the Merrill Woolen Mills. That was a special place to buy wonderful, high-quality clothing and blankets – if there were funds available for such purchases (theirs was a cash-only household), they always chose to shop there.

We had such fun together! I remember Gramma made me a special sundress – off the shoulder in white pique – for a school project, and we took photos in her garden. I was also her assistant at Thanksgiving – a major event in our small family. My job was to make the hard sauce for the mince pie, and I sat on a stool beside the stove, stirring and stirring and stirring for what seemed like hours until the butter and sugar were smooth and 'just right.' She cooked by instinct and seldom measured – one reason why I probably didn't pick it up, though I do have a few recipes in her hand that I cherish. She did have a 'heavy hand' with the alcohol – the 'hard' part of the sauce. She didn't drink herself but was generous with her portions and made sure she set aside some non-alcoholic sauce for herself and me.

And Gramma knew the value of a dollar, too. I've no idea what my grandpa's salary was but every week she divided up his cash pay into her brown manila envelopes. There were quite a few envelopes: one for his clothing, one for hers, another for household expenses, their car, the vacation cottage…and each pay period she spread the wealth. Nothing was purchased unless there was money for it. One exception was when my Grandpa cashed in AT&T stock to send my mom to college for two years during the Depression. Not many women were so fortunate to have parents who saw the value of higher education at that time – and who willingly used their few assets for their only daughter.

One funny story about their cash household was when I was ten or eleven, I went with Grandpa when he bought a new Buick – with cash, of course. It was a 'four-holer' – the largest of the Buick sedans, which all had holes on the side of the front fender. The new car was too long to fit in the garage they rented up the street, so Grandpa drove it back and exchanged it for a 'three-holer' that was a bit shorter. Imagine that kind of a transaction today – and imagine living without credit. They did it, and to my eyes, they had everything they could possibly need or want. No doubt there were challenges, but Gramma was on the case – always.

Gramma was a poised and confident woman – she exuded strength – but she was soft and kind at the same time. She laughed and smiled often. She was very smart, although she only finished high school, and seemed to me to know SO much. She was always responsive to me, even while busy making jam or 'putting up' vegetables from the garden, or tying a rag rug with odd pieces of fabric (including several of Grandpa's old ties which he spotted walking across the rug in their dining room!). I wish I had that rug now!

When my Grandpa died at age 74, Gramma was devastated. They had been married for 54 years, and she hardly recalled life without him. Through the years Gramma had collected antiques, from Grandpa's family and through her travels in the Midwest. Mom and I knew very little about the history of the pieces, so we came up with a 'busy work' project to help Gramma through her mourning period. It turned out to be a genius move, as she really got into it, and to this day, I have her 5x8 notebook with pages of typed notes she made describing, room by room, everything in her home. In her notes, she cited origins, what she paid if she bought something, what she put into it (recovering, refinishing, etc.) and her estimation of its worth.

As Gramma downsized in her retirement home, some of her things came to my mom and me, and at one point I had an insurance appraisal at my home. I sent Gramma a copy of the report to show her just what the value was decades after she jotted down information about her collections. She was amazed but skeptical that something she got free or for less than $100 could possibly be worth thousands of dollars – even in the fluctuating furniture market!

Today I have the daybed I slept on in Gramma's living room, the chest-on-chest that still smells of her dining room – and many other things that are daily reminders of what a truly remarkable woman she was. And I have created a legacy project of my own, so the history of Gramma's collection, and things I've added, is now shared with my kids.

I miss her every day and feel blessed to have so many photos and remembrances of her in my life.

Judy Freshman
Arlington, Virginia

CHAPTER XXX

Mormor ("Mother's mother" in Swedish)
and her granddaughter, Elizabeth

Maja Elisabet

Date of Birth: October 28, 1923. Not deceased.

Maternal Grandmother

Mormor

My Swedish grandparents lived a long airplane ride away, but I have been fortunate to have great memories of and visits with them. I have traveled to Sweden at least fifteen times, beginning when I was around six months old to the present day. My grandparents traveled to the United States many times as well for Christmas holidays, christenings, and general visits. Mormor's last trip to the United States was in August 1995. She still travels regionally but prefers day trips with her friends.

Memories of my grandmother, "Mormor" ("mother's mother" in Swedish), begin at about three years of age. I would travel at least biennially to visit them in Kristianstad, Sweden. My mother was their only child. I am one of three children, but I visited the most. I was the only one who picked up the Swedish language conversationally, as my grandparents spoke only Swedish to me. I can recall only two times my grandmother used English with me. Once when I was five or six, she told me not to touch the stove; it was "Hot." The other time occurred when I was much older – when showing her pictures of my scuba- diving adventures, we came across a picture I took of a nurse shark, and she asked me if I was afraid of "*haj*"(pronounced "hi"). I did not understand the Swedish word, so in English she said, "Shark." I thought, *"See, Mormor, I know you understand so much more English than you let on!"* The first time I can recall speaking in full Swedish was when I was about three years old. My recollection was that during one of my visits, I awoke one morning, put on my red robe, and walked out into the kitchen and said something to Mormor in Swedish. I recall surprised looks on my grandparents' faces, but that might just be a child's memory elaboration. My mom believes that I inherited from Mormor the ability to mimic different voices and sounds. Her storytelling (gentle gossiping, perhaps?) is very entertaining. Mormor also speaks Danish and some German, but still tries to lead us to believe that she is not conversant in English.

"Morfar" ("mother's father") and Mormor lived in a lovely single-level home, which they renovated with a beautiful garden. They had cobblestones laid to outline the gardens, stone walls on the perimeter, and a corner partially enclosed by tall hedges. On nice days, this was where we would have afternoon coffee together. Mormor had an enviable garden in which anything she planted grew beautifully, thanks to her green thumb and the excellent soil conditions. The garden had fruits, herbs and beautiful flowers. I recall cleaning currants, gooseberries, plums and pears to make jams and dessert soups. She also grew rhubarb from which she would remove the huge, thick leaves and then prepare the stalks to make rhubarb dessert soup. This was served with a tablespoon of cream or milk and so delicious, warm or cold. When cooking savory meals requiring herbs, it was my job to go out to the garden to pick the huge dill and parsley stems, which were almost the size of bushes. Another job for me was when we were traveling to someone's house to visit, we would bring a gift which was a Swedish tradition. Mormor would send me out to the garden to pick any flowers of my choosing and make a gift bouquet—roses, catmint, daisies, iris, etc. She never re-adjusted my bouquet, simply wrapped the ends in wet paper towel and foil and had me tie a pretty ribbon. She made me feel proud of my floral arrangements.

Each summer I visited as a little girl, my grandparents would ensure the expected toys were taken down from the attic and ready for play. A doll, doll bed (with clean starched linens), sand/bath toys and my favorite stuffed animal, "Tiger" (which was a lion). As a toddler, I called the lion "Tiger," and from then on, my grandparents called him "Tiger" too. I can remember as a young girl putting Mormor's curlers in Tiger's mane. I don't recall when Tiger was sent back with me to the States, but I still have Tiger. He is on a shelf…to preserve his mane.

Mormor was a very good cook and an excellent hostess. Oh, I envy her gravy-making skill; and her Swedish pancakes and sauces were something that I could never duplicate. During some visits, Mormor, Morfar and I would go "*ut på landet*" (out in the countryside) for strawberry-picking. I think my grandparents had to pay double as my picking method was "one berry in the basket, two in my mouth, one basket, two mouth…" Those sweet, delicious strawberries! Afterwards, we would head home, clean the berries and make jams and sauces. Mormor would put some sauce and cooked berries in a bowl or mug as my evening treat. I called it "*jordgubbe soppa*" (strawberry soup).

Lunch in Sweden is more like a dinner, as it is the main meal of the day. Each summer visit, among my requested menu items was "*stekt sill*" (fried herring). Mormor taught me how to clean, soak, bread and fry the herring. During the meal, my grandparents would have to stop me from eating all of it—*stekt sill* with potatoes and a little cream on the side was so good! At night when we had our evening meal of simple sandwiches, I would ask for more herring (and then fruit soup, of course).

Baking was one of the things I looked forward to when I visited Mormor. We would bake cookies, rolls, and *"mandel skorpor"* (almond biscotti) to have with afternoon coffee or for snacks. Mormor's cinnamon raisin rolls were always available. We would prepare the dough in the morning, let it rise, then fill and roll with butter, sugar, cinnamon and raisins. Early on, I tended to use a little too much of ALL the ingredients—again, Mormor never amended my measurements. "Yes, they are good. Into the oven...'hot.'" [I think my grandfather was being kind when he said my rolls were the best ever—though likely too much filling.]

Every afternoon, Mormor, Morfar and I would have coffee/tea together and enjoy the baked goods. If the weather was nice, we would sit at the little café table in the garden, set with a perfectly starched tablecloth and lovely cups and plates. Even when I visit her as an adult, she is insistent on nice table settings—sometimes simple, but always clean and fresh. From Mormor and my mother, I have learned to set decorative tables, even themed settings. Mormor has given me many of her tablecloths to add to my growing collection and I, too, have diligently starched, pressed and hung them up, ready for the next décor opportunity. Mormor is fastidious and very organized. Even recently, I called her to say hello, and she shared that she was organizing her linen closet—um, it was never disorganized! I hope to achieve that level of neatness one day.

Mormor was a stickler for proper manners and etiquette—everything from thank-you notes to table manners. Classic Mormor remark was offered if one of us stretched our arms at the dinner table: "Ingen gymnastik vid bordet" (no gymnastics at the table). Even today, my siblings and I joke and say that Mormor did not tolerate poor eating manners. We do a light parody of Mormor's dining manners: place napkin in lap, cut food with fork and knife, chew with mouth closed, gracefully tap mouth corners with napkin, and then gracefully sip water. Even joking around, we know these table manners and skills stuck to all of us. Both grandparents would remind us that if you practice when at home, you won't have to think about it when you are eating out.

While my grandmother is very proper, she also has a fun side. For instance, at age 91, she shared that she was getting a walker with wheels and a seat for when she walks in the city squares. When Mormor requested a red walker, the group that distributed them said she could receive a gray one, not a red one. Well, Mormor wanted a red one…and she got a red one. We'll say she is "determined."

Mormor also has a good sense of humor and doesn't shock so easily. For instance, her "TV glasses" for watching TV are not traditional—black glasses that angle up on the sides, with lots of rhinestones. These are a bit different from the conservative style she has—think Queen Elizabeth sans hat. Mormor is not shy; she will talk with anyone and has a very quick wit. Mormor was a great dancer. When Morfar would turn on big band music, Mormor would come to the den, kick off her shoes and show me "what dancing is supposed to look like." I recall an evening when Morfar played a record with Strauss' "Blue Danube" waltz. Mormor danced with Morfar to show me how a lady is supposed to dance the waltz.

My grandparents, though conservative in many ways, had eclectic home design tastes and were artistically talented in different ways. Mormor made pottery figurines, and Morfar painted, sculpted and hammered designs into copper, among their artistic talents. Even their home décor was elegant but diverse. In between the den and the kitchen, there was a small room, more of a nook, with just enough room to place two love seats facing each other, with a glass coffee table in between – it was as if one were comfortably sitting in a train compartment. We occasionally had coffee set up there on rainy days.

Mormor was in her early 20s when she married Morfar, and a few years later my mother was born. They lived in Lund, Sweden, until my mom was a teenager. For my grandfather's job, they moved two hours north to Kristianstad and remained there until my grandfather's passing in November 1988. Mormor then moved back south to Malmö where she currently resides. Mormor is now 93 and will proudly round up to the next year when discussing her age. She still hosts friends for meals or afternoon coffee and will help those who are twenty years her junior!

Mormor is very generous and affectionate. I recall us hugging in towels to warm up after a dip (a *brief* dip) in the cold waters of the Baltic Sea at a beach called Åhus. I have pictures of us hugging, which she captioned *"Mormor's Sommarflicka"* (Mormor's Summer Girl). A few visits ago, she went through her albums and extracted pictures for each of her three grandchildren. I have nearly two albums full of pictures, starting with my christening onto high school.

My husband I were married less than a year when he met Mormor. Through a supposed language barrier and my translation services, each understood the other. The classic memory of their meeting (duplicated each visit) was after the first meal with my grandmother. She opened a very nice cognac, poured two snifters and motioned to my husband to take one. She and my husband did a proper *skål* (toast/cheers). There is a protocol for this as taught to me by my grandparents, and to my husband by me. Afterward, my grandmother sighs and says, "Jar är Viking!" ("I am Viking"). This is now a fun tradition between Mormor and my husband.

When my daughter was four months old, we traveled to see my grandmother. My mother was visiting as well, so I now have an amazing picture of four generations of girls. We returned when she was four years old, and my son was one year old. This past summer, in 2016, we visited again. My daughter was eight and my son was five. I'm so happy that the kids now have real, formidable memories of the visit and can truly say they know "Mormor Maja."

In Sweden, great grandmothers are generally called "*Gamla Mormo*r" (literally translates to "Old Mother's Mother"). Well, Mormor didn't like that ("sounds old"), so we went with "Mormor Maja." Each time I talk to her, she reminisces about the visits, all the hugs and kisses from my kids, and requests more pictures. She has intentionally chosen not to jump into the digital age with cell phones, texting, internet, email, so we are sharing the original way—mail.

Mormor is stoic, independent, strong and active. She is and has been a wonderful model of love, patience, determination and pragmatism. My hope is to emulate these traits and pass them on to my children.

Elizabeth H.
Washington, DC

CHAPTER XXXI

Babushka

Vera Bogomolova

Date of Birth: July 8, 1935. Not deceased.

Maternal Grandmother

Babushka

Enchanting, irresistible, inventive, impassioned, intransigent, indefatigable, incredibly trustworthy, incessantly depriving herself of everything for the comfort and well-being of the others, insanely generous and caring - it's all about her, my maternal grandmother, my *babushka*, my *Verusha*. My iron pole on which I would lean and will never fall, my old well to which I would run to quench my thirst, the shoulder on which I would cry, and would always feel comforted to carry on.

She was born in 1935, in a small village in Georgia (at that time part of the Soviet Union), to where her mother had to escape following turbulent times of the new Post-Revolutionary Era. New orders had split their once big and happy clan and scattered its members across the vast territory of the Soviet Union. It was simply safe to forget the roots and learn to be happy in that new reality. With the inherent sense of humor and Christian patience, my ancestors managed to do that pretty well with no visible dramas or regrets. It was their country they loved and one they wanted to keep on living in.

When I think of my grandma, of all the hardships, deprivations, reforms, losses, deaths, and wars, she and our family had to go through, in this world's biggest country that knew no respite throughout its long history, I realize that these are the things that cemented her character forever. They made her tough and resistant - a tiny lady with a piercing look of her ice-blue eyes. The look that could reverse tides, open any doors and make mountains speak.

At the age of twenty she married a young marine officer, my grandfather, her first and only love. After a modest wedding, they both moved from the South to the North of the Soviet Union behind the Polar Circle, to Murmansk. There, my grandfather started working on small fishing boats, where my mom was born and where they lived all their life until 1987, when my grandfather died. If this is true that behind every great man there is always a great woman, then my grandparents prove this axiom over and above. My grandmother could take credit for all the State awards my grandfather got as a renowned Soviet marine captain-director during his lifetime and for the fact that the biggest fishing trawler of the Russian Northern fleet was given his name after his death. Behind all his victories there were always her sleepless nights, her immense support and hard work.

I am lucky to keep their handwritten letters, a beautiful chronicle of their relationship. I guess because of those tender epistolary style, everybody in the family, including myself, always called my grandma by her first name and its derivatives - *Vera, Verochka, Verusha*.

In those early days in the North, among the post-WWII scarcity of food and clothes, and general poverty so well known to most young couples just starting their lives, she was creating beauty out of nothing. She rebuilt herself, her style, her fashion having payed tribute to her own grandmother, to her noble origins. She introduced timeless western chic in that kingdom of ice, Northern Lights and non-existence, having earned a reputation of the most elegant captain's spouse.

She taught the art of sewing to the little girls in the North, but more than that she taught them style. "Always respect yourself. Remember who you are", she used to repeat. I am proud I am one of her students and happy that her unique DNA lives in the collections of clothes we started making together and still keep on doing up to this day.

I have never heard her complaining about anything. Once on a train trip we had to share a four place standard compartment with a very rowdy retired military general. He was carrying a huge old fashioned TV set with him on an upper berth, risking to drop it on our heads every time the train was making a stop. After a long dispute, my grandmother pierced the general with her ice-blue eyes and took the decision. For two nights she was sleeping squeezed between the huge TV box and the bags to keep me safe. At the end of the trip we got off at our station and the general continued. I will never forget his astonished eyes as he was looking through the window of the carriage at this stylish tiny lady in black stilettos hopping over the rails holding in one hand three bags and in the other one the hand of her little granddaughter.

I remember so well all those train trips: the summer ones to the South of the country to the Black Sea and the winter ones to the North of the country to the Barents Sea. Each of them was two-three day long and in its own way was a little ritual. Among numerous suitcases and boxes, there was a huge bag full of homemade food: a big glass jar with fresh hot chicken-noodle soup or *bor*sch with a mind-blowing smell that made people from the other compartments peep through our door, minced meat cutlets with mashed potatoes and her famous apple-cowberry pies.

Still now, she and I are as thick as thieves. But in those train trip days back in the 80-90s, we were especially close. In those days, at the fracture of the epochs, when the Soviet Union was no longer there by the Russia we know today was not there either, when all human qualities, good or bad, were being tested at their extremes.

New winds of changes brought her back to her roots to the South to finally settle down and start building a new home to mark our family nest. She naturally converted herself from a stylist and a fashion icon into an avid gardener and an architect easily managing a handful of stubborn builders.

In 2015, we inaugurated our new family nest and almost at the same time my twins were born. When I first looked at my newborn daughter I could not believe it… my little bundle looked exactly like my grandmother - the same color of the eyes and the same heart-shape nose. There was no question the little girl's first name would be Vera.

It was that same year when we all got together to celebrate the 80th birthday of my grandmother in the new house. The Big Vera and the Little Verushka were sitting together at a big festive table under the high white arches and the full moon was looking down at them through the tall windows.

"God save us from all wars", whispered my grandmother and tears sparkled in her eyes as she looked over to her little great-grand-daughter. "No more wars…please."

We all clinked our glasses.

Natasha de Francisco
Washington, DC